Power Words Copymasters

A Bridge to Reading

McDougal Littell

BRIDGES TO

LITERATURE

LEVEL I

by
William McBride, Ph.D.

McDougal Littell
A HOUGHTON MIFFLIN COMPANY

Evanston, Illinois • Boston • Dallas

ISBN-13: 978-0-618-36409-1   ISBN-10: 0-618-36409-9

Printed in the United States of America.

6 7 8 9−MDO−09 08 07 06

Table of Contents

Vocabulary Instruction for Older Students
by William McBride, Ph.D.

Teachers in middle and high schools today are faced with a number of students who are unable to read their textbooks. One way teachers can help their students improve reading comprehension is through direct vocabulary instruction. Comprehension is an active process in which students connect what they already know to information in a text. Research in the past decade has shown that direct vocabulary instruction has a significant effect on improving comprehension (Laflamme, 1997). This instructional workbook is designed to provide classroom teachers with the tools they need to help students become better readers through vocabulary development.

What Works

A number of strategies have been proven to be effective in helping students decode or understand words in texts (Blachowicz, C. & Lee, John, 1991; Ivey, G. & Broaddus, K., 1999; Moats, 2001; Stahl, S., 1999, Vacca & Vacca, 1993). Researchers recommend that teachers use the following strategies:
- Extensive reading at a child's independent reading level
- Instruction in the sound-symbol relationships in words (phonics)
- Instruction in word meanings
- Instruction in using context to derive meaning
- Instruction in morphology (roots, prefixes, and suffixes)
- Instruction in idiomatic expressions
- Practice in fluent reading
- Fun, interactive activities

Lesson Development

Power Words: A Bridge to Reading is designed to provide the types of instruction that are cited in the above research. The program has three levels. Each level is divided into twelve units. Each unit has three lessons and a unit test. The lessons are structured in the following format:

1. **Prior Knowledge/Oral Language:** Lessons begin by accessing students' prior knowledge. Students are prompted to share what they may already know about the lesson's target words. In some cases target words have multiple meanings. To help students understand multiple meanings, draw out as many meanings of a word as students are able to produce. For example, one student may define the word *current* as a noun (the current in the river) while another defines it as an adjective (a current newspaper).

2. **Power Words List:** Lessons 1 and 2 each introduce twelve target words to students. Lesson 3 reviews and reteaches the twenty-four words from the previous two lessons. The criteria for selecting target words in each lesson are as follows:
   - Words that exemplify the particular skills being taught
   - Words that are commonly found on standardized tests
   - Words that are taught in McDougal Littell's *Bridges to Literature* program

3. **Instruction and Exercises:** Each lesson in a unit provides instruction and practice with <u>three</u> different skills. For example, Lesson 1 may cover synonyms, Latin and Greek roots, and context clues. One page of instruction and practice is devoted to each skill. Brain-based teaching methods reinforce the need for reteaching of concepts (Jensen, 1998; Sprenger, 1999). Consequently, Lesson 2 reteaches the same skills covered in Lesson 1, but with a new group of twelve target words. Finally, because students need multiple opportunities to learn how words are conceptually related (Vacca & Vacca, 1993), Lesson 3 reviews the previously taught twenty-four target words and, for a third time, reteaches the three skills covered in the unit.

4. **Skill Instruction:** The following skills are taught in every level of *Power Words: A Bridge to Reading*. Please note that most of these skills are covered multiple times within any one level. For example, in Level 1, affixes are covered in three separate units and context clues are covered in six separate units. The order of skill instruction for each level matches the skill instruction in McDougal Littell's *Bridges to Literature*.
   • Affixes
   • Compound Words
   • Multiple Meaning Words
   • Greek and Latin Roots
   • Context Clues
   • Shades of Meaning
   • Synonyms and Antonyms
   • Syllabication (through phonics)
   • Structural Analysis
   • Idioms
   • Homophones
   • Specialized Vocabulary
   • Foreign Words
   • Using a Dictionary

5. **Fluency:** Reading fluency is the ability to automatically recognize words. Fluency involves both decoding and comprehension skills. A fluent reader decodes so effortlessly that he or she can concentrate on meaning. Thus a good reader reads more quickly than a less-able reader. Readers can increase their fluency through practice. Consequently, in either Lesson 2 or 3 of every unit an exercise is devoted to fluency. Teachers can group students in pairs and have them practice reading to each other in "two-foot voices." Students can time each other and note errors, working towards correct, smooth readings.

6. **Unit Tests:** Each unit ends with a three-page test to evaluate students' knowledge of the target words and skills taught. The Unit Tests are designed to look like the test items on major standardized tests used in this country. Many items on standardized tests are written in formats that students do not see in normal reading tests. By exposing students to these formats, students are able to practice their test-taking skills.

7. **Answer Keys:** In the back of each level you will find Answer Keys for both the Lessons and the Unit Tests. For your information, a copy of the Dolch Basic Sight Word List has also been included. Students must know these words automatically to become fluent readers.

Instructional Plan for *Power Words*

You may want to follow the instructional plan described below.

Week 1 - Monday – Incorporate a highly-successful activity called Word Wall (Cunningham, P. 2000). Either write the twelve words from *Power Words* Lesson 1 on the board or cut out large construction paper "bricks" and put the words on the wall. At the start of class, ask students to number a sheet of paper from one to twelve. As an oral activity, call out the first word and ask if anyone in the class knows its meaning and how he or she knows it. If no one knows the word, use the word in a sentence that provides enough context so that students can discern its definition. Come to a group decision as to the best definition of the word, write the definition on the board and have students copy it down. You may have one student look up the word in a dictionary, select the definition that fits the way the word is used in the sentence, and read the definition aloud. Continue until all twelve words are defined. Spend the rest of the period with regular activities. If you are using McDougal Littell's high interest/low readability series *Bridges to Literature,* begin the first selection in the unit.

Tuesday – Begin the class with Word Wall by calling out the definitions from Monday and have students copy the correct word from the wall. In this way, students are practicing the correct spellings while learning the definitions. Pass out *Power Words* Lesson 1 Worksheets and guide students through the three pages of activities to make sure they understand the format of each exercise. If time allows, continue with regular literature-based activities. In *Bridges,* use the SkillBuilder sheets related to the selection you read the day before.

Wednesday – Begin the class with Word Wall by calling out the definitions. Then review the answers to the Lesson 1 exercises. Finish class with your regular literature-based activities. In *Bridges,* finish the first selection and move to the second.

Thursday – Before students arrive, add the twelve words from *Power Words* Lesson 2 to your Word Wall. Follow Monday's procedure of having students define the new words and copy the definitions. Continue with your regular activities. In *Bridges,* finish the second selection and any Skillbuilder worksheets.

Friday – Begin the class with Word Wall, calling out the definitions of ALL twenty-four words as the students write the correct word. Finish the class with regular literature-based activities or move to the third story in *Bridges.*

Week 2 - Monday – Begin the class with Word Wall, calling out all twenty-four words from the previous week. Then distribute *Power Words* Lesson 2 Worksheets. Guide students through the activities. Students should be able to work more independently on these lessons as these skills are the same skills taught in Lesson 1.

Tuesday – Begin the class with Word Wall with all twenty-four words. Review the answers to the Lesson 2 Worksheets. Finish the class with regular literature-based activities. In *Bridges,* move into the fourth selection if applicable or finish any activities from previous selections covered.

Wednesday – Begin the class with Word Wall with all twenty-four words. Pass out *Power Words* Lesson 3 Worksheets, which reviews the skills and words taught in the first two lessons. Guide students through these activities. Allow students to take Lesson 3 home to study with an adult in the home. Finish the class with regular literature-based activities. In *Bridges,* finish covering the literature and SkillBuilder sheets in the unit. Tell students to study their *Power Words* for a test on Friday.

Thursday – Begin the class with Word Wall with all twenty-four words. Review the answers to the Lesson 3 Worksheets. Finish the class with regular literature-based activities.

Friday – Pass out the *Power Words* Unit Test. Because parts of the test resemble test items on major standardized tests, you may want to explain variations in format for certain test items. Count the test as a major grade and place it in the student's portfolio.

Bibliography

Billmeyer, R. & Barton, M. (1998). *Teaching Reading in the Content Areas: If Not Me, Then Who?* Aurora, CO: McREL.

Blachowicz, C., & Lee, J. (November, 1991). Vocabulary development in the whole literacy classroom. *The Reading Teacher, 45 (3), 188–194.*

Cunningham, P. (2000). *Phonics They Use: Words for Reading and Writing* (3rd ed.) New York: Longman.

Ivey, G., & Broaddus, K. (1991). 1700+ students speak out about middle school reading. Paper presented at the 49th annual meeting of the National Reading Conference, Orlando, FL.

Jensen, Eric. (1998). *Teaching with the Brain in Mind.* Alexandria, VA: ASCD.

Laflamme, J.G. (1997). The effect of the Multiple Exposure Vocabulary Method and the Target Reading/Writing Strategy on test scores. *Journal of Adolescent and Adult Literacy, 40 (5), 372–381.*

Micklos, J. & Freeman, M. (Eds.). (Aug./Sept., 2002) Examining Evidence: New IRA position statement on evidence-based reading instruction lists practices proven effective by valid research. *Reading Today 20 (1).*

Moats, Louisa C., (March, 2001). When Older Students Can't Read. *Educational Leadership.* (pp. 36–40) Alexandria, VA: ASCD.

Sprenger, Marilee. (1999). *Learning and Memory: The Brain in Action.* Alexandria, VA: ASCD.

Stahl, S. (1986). Three principles of effective vocabulary instruction. *Journal of Reading, 29, 662–671.*

Stahl, S. (Stahl, Steven. (1999). *Vocabulary Development.* Cambridge, MA: Brookline Books.

Vacca, R.T., & Vacca, J.L. (1993). Content Area Reading (4th ed.). New York: Harper Collins.

Name _____   Date _____

Power Words

Look at the words below. Circle any that you think you may know. Be ready to tell the class what the word means. Also tell the class how you think you know that word.

dustpan	preshunk	ravenous	splendid
froze	preview	retook	trouble
ghastly	pullover	sorehead	unbound

Part 1: Synonyms

Words that have nearly the same meaning are called **synonyms**. For example, **greedy** and **money-loving** both mean about the same thing. These two words are synonyms.

A. Darken the circle for the word from the list that is a synonym of the **bold-faced** word in the sentence.

1. The king thought his daughter was **splendid** because she could cook and sew.
   - ○ silly
   - ○ wonderful
   - ○ stupid
   - ○ lazy

2. King Midas was **ravenous** because all of his food had turned to gold.
   - ○ sleepy
   - ○ talkative
   - ○ hungry
   - ○ powerful

3. Everything the king touched **froze** in place.
   - ○ stopped
   - ○ tasted
   - ○ ran
   - ○ fell

4. The king knew he was in **trouble** when he was unable to eat.
   - ○ time
   - ○ difficulty
   - ○ pain
   - ○ joy

5. Midas was glad when the **ghastly** wish was gone.
   - ○ nice
   - ○ helpful
   - ○ pretty
   - ○ terrible

Unit 1, Lesson 1

Part 2: Prefixes and Base Words

A **base word** is a word that can stand alone. A **prefix** is a word part added to the beginning of a base word. For example, in the word **retry**, *try* is the base word and *re-* is the prefix added at the beginning. The spelling of the base word does not change when adding a prefix. Knowing the meaning of a prefix helps you figure out the meaning of the whole word. *Retry* means "to try again." Study the meaning of the following prefixes until you can remember what each means.

un- means "not" or "the opposite of"
re- means "again" or "back"
pre- means "before"

A. Draw a line between the base word and the prefix for each word below. Then write what the word means on the line.

1. unequal - _____

2. replay - _____

3. preview - _____

4. unable - _____

5. retry - _____

6. preshrunk - _____

7. unfair - _____

8. retook - _____

9. pretest - _____

10. unbound - _____

B. Choose the correct word to complete each sentence.

unconscious   recount   preschool   uncertain   repossess

1. We were not sure who won the election so we had to _____ the votes.

2. The worker fell off the building, hit his head, and lay on the ground _____ .

3. My little sister is too young for school so she goes to _____ .

4. The bank came to _____ the car when the young man could not pay for it.

5. I didn't study for the test so I was _____ about the correct answers.

Unit 1, Lesson 1

Part 3: Compound Words

A **compound word** is a word made by putting two words together. Knowing the meaning of the smaller words helps you figure out the meaning of the whole word. For example, **fishbowl** is made of the smaller words *fish* and *bowl*. You can figure out that a fishbowl is a bowl in which fish live.

A. Combine each word in **Row 1** with a word in **Row 2** to make a compound word. Then write each compound word beside its definition below.

Row 1:   basket   flash   dust   pull   sore

Row 2:   pan   head   ball   light   over

1. someone who is angry or easily offended   _____

2. a small, portable lamp or light   _____

3. a short-handled pan to scoop up dirt   _____

4. a ball used in a popular sport   _____

5. a sweater or sweatshirt   _____

B. Use a compound word from Exercise A to complete the following sentences. Then, see if you can find the other compound word in each sentence and circle it.

1. The bedroom was so dark that we needed a _____ to see.

2. My grandmother told me to take a _____ in case I got cold.

3. Steven is not a fun partygoer. He's always such a _____.

4. Next to football, _____ is another sport I love.

5. Ricardo threw the dirt from the _____ outdoors.

6. David is a real _____ when he loses at any ballgame.

7. Our high school's _____ team scored 104 points the other night!

8. We lost our _____ so we used a piece of newspaper to clean the floor.

9. The park ranger uses a _____ to spot bears in the campground.

10. It was cold at the ballpark so we took a _____.

Unit 1, Lesson 2

Power Words

Look at the words below. Circle any that you think you may know. Be ready to tell the class what the word means. Also tell the class how you think you know that word.

comfortable	lawman	original	sustainable
deceived	mythical	pinprick	tread
lawful	notion	priceless	underdog

Part 1: Synonyms

Words that have nearly the same meaning are called **synonyms**. For example, **angry** and **mad** have nearly the same meaning. These words are synonyms.

A. Read the sentences below. Use the words and ideas in the sentence to help you figure out what the word in **bold** means. Then find a synonym for the bold word in the choices below. Darken in the circle of the correct choice.

1. Alfred was **deceived** when the girl with the green ribbon didn't tell him the truth.
   - ○ welcomed
   - ○ taxed
   - ○ fooled
   - ○ told

2. The turtle had a strange **notion** that he could fly.
   - ○ story
   - ○ idea
   - ○ program
   - ○ sickness

3. The boy had an **original** idea that no one had thought of concerning the dead fish.
   - ○ fresh
   - ○ difficult
   - ○ sad
   - ○ awful

4. The story of the turtle and the swans is a **mythical** one that couldn't happen in real life.
   - ○ forgotten
   - ○ deadly
   - ○ real
   - ○ imaginary

5. The boy **tread** carefully as he entered his neighbors house.
   - ○ stepped
   - ○ talked
   - ○ slept
   - ○ ate

Name _____   Date _____

Part 2: Suffixes and Base Words

You remember that a **base word** is a word that can stand alone. A **suffix** is a word part added to the end of a base word. For example, the word **helpful** is made up of the base word **help** and the suffix **-ful**. Knowing the meaning of a suffix helps you figure out the meaning of the whole word. *Helpful* means someone who is full of help. Study the meaning of the following suffixes until you can remember what each means.

-ful means "full of" or "having"
-able means "wanting to" or "able to be"
-less means "without" or "lacking"

A. Draw a line between the base word and the suffix for each word below. Then write what the word means on the line. Use a dictionary if necessary.

1. comfortable - _____

2. joyful - _____

3. breathless - _____

4. truthful - _____

5. priceless - _____

6. moveable - _____

7. fearful - _____

8. endless - _____

9. sustainable - _____

10. thoughtful - _____

B. Add a suffix to each base word to create a word with the meaning shown. Then write a short sentence using each new word.

1. agree_____; wanting to please _____

2. youth_____; young and alive _____

3. pain_____; without hurt _____

4. replace_____; able to put back _____

5. law_____; legal and proper _____

Unit 1, Lesson 2

Part 3: Compound Words

A compound word is a word made by putting two words together. Knowing the meaning of the smaller words helps you figure out the meaning of the whole word. For example, playground is made of the smaller words "play" and "ground." You can figure out that playground is a place for people to play.

A. Combine these pairs of words to make compound words. Write the compound word and what you think it means on the line. Use a dictionary to check your answers.

1. jail + break _____

2. ground + out _____

3. over + spend _____

4. pin + prick _____

5. scare + crow _____

6. stink + bug _____

7. crash + worthy _____

8. law + man _____

9. sand + castle _____

10. under + dog _____

B. Fluency: There are 14 words from this lesson in the following story. Circle all the words you can find. Then practice reading the story until you can read it smoothly.

My grandmother was not very joyful when I told her I had a new skateboard. In

fact, she was rather coarse with me. She said to me, "John, I have to be truthful. I

know it is lawful to ride your skateboard, but I don't think they are very crashwor-

thy. I'm very fearful when you go out in the street on that thing."

"But grandmother," I said. "I didn't overspend my allowance for it. I know you're

not comfortable with me riding it, but life is so dull without it."

Grandmother said, "John, I realize this is a youthful thing to do, but if you fall it

will not be painless. Would you at least be thoughtful and stay out of traffic?"

"Okay," I said, feeling pretty low. "I will be agreeable and careful for you."

Unit 1, Lesson 3

Power Words Review

Look at the words below. Circle any that you think you may know. Be ready to tell the class what the word means. Also tell the class how you think you know that word.

comfortable	lawman	preview	splendid
deceived	mythical	priceless	sustainable
dustpan	notion	pullover	tread
froze	original	ravenous	trouble
ghastly	pinprick	retook	unbound
lawful	preshrunk	sorehead	underdog

Part 1: Synonyms

You have learned that words with nearly the same meaning are called **synonyms**. For example, **rich** and **wealthy** are synonyms.

A. Write a synonym for the **boldfaced** words on the line provided. The answers are in the **Power Words Review** from above. Use a dictionary or a thesaurus if needed.

1. Juan had **difficulty** with the test in math class.   _____

2. I felt **hungry** as soon as I smelled the pizza.   _____

3. Sarah was **fooled** when her friend lied to her.   _____

4. I **stopped** in my tracks when I saw the ghost.   _____

5. Sarah had a **fresh** idea as to how to solve the problem.   _____

6. The person in the car wreck had some **terrible** injuries.   _____

7. The story was an **imaginary** one of a talking turtle.   _____

8. We had a **wonderful** time on vacation.   _____

9. I **stepped** lightly so as not to wake my mother.   _____

10. Juan had a great **idea** for a new football play.   _____

Unit 1, Lesson 3

Part 2: Prefixes and Suffixes

Affixes are word parts added to base words. A **prefix** is added to the beginning of a base word. A **suffix** is added to the end of a base word.

A. For each example in Column A, draw a line between the affix and the base word. Then match each example in Column A with its correct meaning in Column B. Write the letter of the correct meaning in the space provided. Use a dictionary if necessary.

Column A

1. comfortable _____
2. retry _____
3. thoughtful _____
4. preview _____
5. unfair _____
6. endless _____
7. agreeable _____
8. preschool _____
9. repossess _____
10. replaceable _____

Column B

A. to think about or care for others

B. a school for very young children

C. to take back

D. pleasurable, providing comfort

E. can be replaced

F. easy to get along with, pleasant

G. to attempt or try again

H. not fair or reasonable

I. going on forever; without end

J. to look at or see before others do

B. Add one of the affixes listed below to the list of words. Write the new word on the line provided. You can use each affix only once.

un   able   re   less   ful   pre

1. shrunk: _____
2. price: _____
3. equal: _____
4. play: _____
5. sustain: _____
6. truth: _____

Part 3: Compound Words

As you know, a **compound word** is made up of two smaller words. The fifteen compound words below are hidden in this word search puzzle. First draw a line between the two words in each compound word. Then find each of the compound words in the puzzle. Words in the puzzle can be written across, up and down, backwards, or diagonally.

BASKETBALL	JAILBREAK	SANDCASTLE
CRASHWORTHY	LAWMAN	SCARECROW
DUSTPAN	OVERSPEND	SOREHEAD
FLASHLIGHT	PINPRICK	STINKBUG
GROUNDOUT	PULLOVER	UNDERDOG

Compound Word Search

```
O V E R S P E N D B P W G U R
K P G I Y R D J T A I O U N L
Q W Y E C U P U V S N R B D R
M J D E S D O D A K P C K E X
C Z P T K D H N G E R E N R P
B R P S N I D O W T I R I D K
K A A U B C E W E B C A T O P
N A O S A G O K J A K C S G B
L R E S H T H G I L H S A L F
G I T R C W K X P L N O H Z X
A L G J B C O D A E H E R O S
E P H D Q L Z R O N A M W A L
M H D A L R I L T S Q J S J U
X M E A I X Z A U H Z K K U G
P U L L O V E R J Z Y S G A L
```

Unit 1, Test

Part A: Synonyms

Directions: Choose the word that means about the same as the underlined word.

1. David was <u>ravenous</u>.
   - ○ mad
   - ○ hungry
   - ○ tricky
   - ○ sick

2. an <u>original</u> idea
   - ○ fresh
   - ○ old
   - ○ bad
   - ○ sad

3. a <u>mythical</u> story
   - ○ interesting
   - ○ silly
   - ○ wonderful
   - ○ imaginary

4. She <u>froze</u> in place.
   - ○ laughed
   - ○ begged
   - ○ stopped
   - ○ slept

5. a <u>ghastly</u> wish
   - ○ nice
   - ○ terrible
   - ○ lovely
   - ○ granted

6. a silly <u>notion</u>
   - ○ model
   - ○ speech
   - ○ idea
   - ○ teacher

7. in <u>trouble</u>
   - ○ difficulty
   - ○ water
   - ○ space
   - ○ bed

8. a <u>splendid</u> meal
   - ○ bad
   - ○ cold
   - ○ wonderful
   - ○ nice

9. Sheila was <u>deceived</u>.
   - ○ glad
   - ○ sorry
   - ○ fooled
   - ○ mad

10. <u>Tread</u> softly.
   - ○ step
   - ○ talk
   - ○ travel
   - ○ work

Unit 1, Test

Part B: Prefixes and Suffixes

Directions: Fill in the letter of the word that most nearly matches the meaning of the underlined word.

1. an <u>unequal</u> fight
   - Ⓐ interesting
   - Ⓑ right
   - Ⓒ truthful
   - Ⓓ not fair
   - Ⓔ sad

2. instant <u>replay</u>
   - Ⓕ game
   - Ⓖ try out
   - Ⓗ play again
   - Ⓘ goal
   - Ⓙ score again

3. We watched a <u>preview</u>.
   - Ⓚ sequel
   - Ⓛ repeat
   - Ⓜ drama
   - Ⓝ comedy
   - Ⓞ early showing

4. The desk was <u>moveable</u>.
   - Ⓟ could be moved
   - Ⓠ worthless
   - Ⓡ old
   - Ⓢ able to be sold
   - Ⓣ could be shared

5. That painting is <u>priceless</u>.
   - Ⓐ worthless
   - Ⓑ costly
   - Ⓒ in bad shape
   - Ⓓ for sale
   - Ⓔ without a frame

6. a <u>breathless</u> dancer
   - Ⓕ tired
   - Ⓖ silly
   - Ⓗ awkward
   - Ⓘ young
   - Ⓙ ballroom

7. an <u>endless</u> drive
   - Ⓚ without direction
   - Ⓛ very easy
   - Ⓜ fast
   - Ⓝ wild
   - Ⓞ never ending

8. a <u>lawful</u> policeman
   - Ⓟ brave
   - Ⓠ full of daring
   - Ⓡ very proper
   - Ⓢ crazy
   - Ⓣ full of humor

9. an <u>unbound</u> prisoner
   - Ⓐ unhappy
   - Ⓑ lifetime
   - Ⓒ sad
   - Ⓓ unafraid
   - Ⓔ untied or free

10. I will <u>repossess</u> your house.
    - Ⓕ share
    - Ⓖ restart
    - Ⓗ sell
    - Ⓘ take back
    - Ⓙ repaint

Unit 1, Test

Part C: Compound Words

Directions: Match the meaning of the compound word in **Column B** with the word in **Column A**. Fill in the letter of the definition on the blank provided.

Column A

1. _____ lawman

2. _____ flashlight

3. _____ sorehead

4. _____ underdog

5. _____ stinkbug

6. _____ dustpan

7. _____ overspend

8. _____ pullover

9. _____ sandcastle

10. _____ crashworthy

11. _____ scarecrow

12. _____ pinprick

13. _____ basketball

14. _____ jailbreak

15. _____ groundout

Column B

A. an escape from prison or jail

B. a sweater or sweatshirt

C. to spend more than one has or wanted to

D. able to withstand a crash or wreck

E. a type of sport

F. a structure built out of sand usually at the beach

G. a hand-held light powered by batteries

H. to hit the ball on the ground and be called out

I. a pan for collecting dirt and dust

J. a hole or wound made by a pin or needle

K. a straw man used to scare birds in a field

L. a bug that gives off a bad smell

M. a police officer

N. someone who is easily angered

O. one expected to lose a contest or fight

Unit 2, Lesson 1

Power Words

Look at the words below. Circle any that you think you may know. Be ready to tell the class what the word means. Also tell the class how you think you know that word.

barren	crept	maze	tardy
canyons	dim	moist	urgently
cellar	hoarse	pail	vertically

Part 1: Antonyms

Words that have nearly opposite meanings are called **antonyms**. For example, **beautiful** and **ugly** mean the opposite of each other. These two words are antonyms.

A. Darken the circle for the word from the list that is an antonym of the **boldfaced** word in the sentence.

1. The canyons were **dry** because of little rain and snow.
   - ○ brown
   - ○ hot
   - ○ sandy
   - ○ moist

2. The strong wind **raced** across the grey seas.
   - ○ sped
   - ○ yelled
   - ○ crept
   - ○ flew

3. The **fertile** field was filled with different vegetables and fruit trees.
   - ○ barren
   - ○ green
   - ○ lush
   - ○ beautiful

4. John is an eager student so he is always **early** for class.
   - ○ quickly
   - ○ quietly
   - ○ loudly
   - ○ tardy

5. The **bright** neon sign punctuates the darkness.
   - ○ red
   - ○ dim
   - ○ old
   - ○ flashing

Unit 2, Lesson 1

Part 2: Homophones

Words that sound the same but have different spellings and meanings are called **homophones**. For example, **tail** and **tale** are homophones. Here are some other examples of homophones.

red and **read**	**break** and **brake**	**horse** and **hoarse**
led and **lead**	**maze** and **maize**	**heal** and **heel** and **he'll**
no and **know**	**flew** and **flu**	**night** and **knight**
pail and **pale**		

A. Decide which of the homophones above answer the questions. Write the correct homophone in the blank. Use a dictionary if necessary.

1. What did the woman do to stop the car? _____

2. How did the sick boy look? _____

3. What is the color of a stop sign? _____

4. What is another name for corn? _____

5. How did the man sound who was losing his voice? _____

6. What does a wound do over time? _____

7. If asked to do drugs, what should you say? _____

8. What is a type of metal? _____

9. What is the opposite of day? _____

10. How did the bird get home? _____

B. Circle the two homophones in each sentence. Write a brief definition of each. Use a dictionary if necessary.

1. The rose was the prettiest flower in the rows of plants.

   _____

2. The rock climber got a peek at the peak of the mountain.

   _____

3. The seller went down to the cellar to get some more products.

   _____

Unit 2, Lesson 1

Part 3: Structural Analysis

Many words have endings added to them that change their meanings. For example, when you add an -s to many nouns, it makes the noun plural. One *tree* changes to many *trees*. Study the chart below to see how the endings change the meanings of words.

Ending	Example	Change
the noun ending *-s*	*car* becomes *car<u>s</u>*	makes one thing more than one, or plural
the participle ending *-ing*	*ride* becomes *rid<u>ing</u>*	describes or shows action
the adverb ending *-ly*	*loud* becomes *loud<u>ly</u>*	tells how something is done

A. Each of the **boldfaced** words in the following sentences has an <u>incorrect</u> ending. Rewrite the boldfaced word correctly on the line provided.

1. The river goes **slides** by. _____

2. The wind made all the **doorly** in the house rattle. _____

3. The star fell very **quicking** through the sky. _____

4. Hold fast to **dreamly** so that you won't lose them. _____

5. When I saw the accident, I called **urgenting** for help. _____

6. The wind raced across the seven great **sealy**. _____

7. A **burns** star is very bright. _____

8. We got lost hiking in the many **canyoning**. _____

9. She sat up **verticals** in bed. _____

10. The boy on the bicycle went **races** down the street. _____

B. With a partner, come up with five **-ing** words that describe a dog and five **-ly** words that tell how you might talk to a friend.

_____   _____
_____   _____
_____   _____
_____   _____
_____   _____

Unit 2, Lesson 2

Power Words

Look at the words below. Circle any that you think you may know. Be ready to tell the class what the word means. Also tell the class how you think you know that word.

absent	genius	knead	soar
adolescent	imperfect	knot	throne
confidence	inspect	obey	whisper

Part 1: Antonyms

Words that have nearly opposite meanings are called **antonyms**. For example, **quiet** and **loud** mean the opposite of each other. These two words are antonyms. Also, remember that synonyms are two words with nearly the same meaning.

A. Decide if the following pairs of words are antonyms or synonyms. In the blank write **A** for Antonym and **S** for Synonym.

1. dark : light   _____

2. absent : missing   _____

3. violent : peaceful   _____

4. innocent : guilty   _____

5. adolescent : teen   _____

6. future : past   _____

7. distant : far   _____

8. confidence : trust   _____

9. excellent : poor   _____

10. obey : revolt   _____

B. Think of an antonym for the following words. Write it in the blank. You may use a dictionary or thesaurus if necessary.

1. whisper : _____ 2. falling : _____

3. rude : _____   4. danger : _____

5. barren : _____   6. genius : _____

Unit 2, Lesson 2

Part 2: Homophones

Words that sound the same but have different spellings and meanings are called **homophones**. For example, **our** and **hour** are homophones.

A. Circle the homophones in each sentence. Then write a brief definition of each homophone on the line provided. Use a dictionary if necessary.

1. I said hi to my neighbor as he climbed the high stairs.

   _____

2. We'll need to take the wheel off of the car to fix the flat.

   _____

3. The high jumper was unable to soar over the bar because of her sore heel.

   _____

4. If you're going to knead the bread, you'll need some flour first.

   _____

5. The medal hanging on his uniform was made of a very rare metal.

   _____

6. The night of the revolt, the king was thrown off of his throne.

   _____

7. Their brothers said they're here in order to visit their friend over there.

   _____

8. I'm not about to get this knot undone.

   _____

9. Jane rode in the boat as her son rowed under the old road bridge.

   _____

10. My mom made the maid a plate of cookies for the holidays.

    _____

Unit 2, Lesson 2

Part 3: Structural Analysis

Many words have endings added to them that change their meanings. For example, when you add *-er* to *play*, the word becomes *player*. The meaning changes to one who does an action. Study the chart below to see how endings change the meanings of words.

Ending	Example	Change
the noun ending *-es*	*beach* becomes *beaches*	shows more than one or plurals
the verb ending *-ed*	*walk* becomes *walked* *bat* becomes *batted*	shows action in the past
the suffixes *-er* and *-or*	*teach* becomes *teacher* *invent* becomes *inventor*	shows one who does or is something

A. Each of the **boldfaced** words in the following sentences is missing an ending. Rewrite the boldfaced word correctly on the line provided.

1. The **teach** spent the day reading to her students.   _____

2. Yesterday the wind **roar** through the trees.   _____

3. Luis couldn't wait to open all the **box**.   _____

4. Debbie **miss** the train because she was late.   _____

5. The **inspect** looked closely at all the cartons of milk.   _____

6. Katasha is a better **read** than most of her classmates.   _____

7. No one likes the different **lunch** served in the cafeteria.   _____

8. Last year Tom **pass** by my class every morning.   _____

9. Jerry was glad he had **cash** his check.   _____

10. Jerome was the best **dance** in the school.   _____

B. Make the following words plural by adding *-s* or *-es*, past tense by adding *-ed*, and a person by adding *-er* or *-or*. Use a dictionary if necessary to check your spelling.

Word	Plural (*-s* or *-es*)	Past Tense (*-ed*)	Person (*-er* or *-or*)
crash			
kiss			
slap			
brush			
bomb			

Unit 2, Lesson 3

Power Words Review

Look at the words below. Circle any that you think you may know. Be ready to tell the class what the word means. Also tell the class how you think you know that word.

absent	crept	knead	soar
adolescent	dim	knot	tardy
barren	genius	maze	throne
canyons	hoarse	moist	urgently
cellar	imperfect	obey	vertically
confidence	inspect	pail	whisper

Part 1: Antonyms

You have learned that words that have nearly opposite meanings are called **antonyms**. For example, **big** and **small** mean the opposite of each other.

A. Write an antonym in the blank for each of the words below. You'll find your answer in the Power Words listed above.

1. adult _____

2. disobey _____

3. scream _____

4. attic _____

5. here _____

6. early _____

7. perfect _____

8. stupid _____

9. dry _____

10. horizontally _____

11. bright _____

12. ran _____

Unit 2, Lesson 3

Part 2: Homophones

Words that sound the same but have different spellings and meanings are called
homophones. For example, **sail** and **sale** are homophones.

A. In the blank provided, write a homophone for each of the words below. Some
words have two homophones. Use a dictionary if necessary.

1. sore   _____

2. wheel   _____

3. led   _____

4. horse   _____

5. brake   _____

6. no   _____

7. thrown   _____

8. made   _____

9. their   _____   _____

10. heal   _____

11. medal   _____

12. road   _____   _____

B. Fluency: Read the story below. There are 18 homophones in the following story;
however, each of them is the wrong word. Circle the incorrect homophone and
write the correct word above it. Then practice reading the story until you can read
it smoothly.

   This is a tail about an old bear who was sick with the flew. The bear had lead his
family to a cave knot far from the rowed. He told his wife that he thought the maze
he had eaten had maid him sick. His wife said, "Well, wheel just sit here until you
are know longer soar. I no you need to rest. You need a brake."

   The bare family weighted until the father began to heel. Finally he felt better. He
told his family, "Everyone in hour family deserves a metal for sticking together."

   The wife and baby bears all blushed and turned bright read.

Part 3: Structural Analysis

Study the word endings and how they change words in the chart below.

Ending	Example	Change
the noun ending -s	*bag* becomes *bags*	makes one thing more than one, or plural
the participle ending -ing	*talk* becomes *talking*	describes or shows action
the adverb ending -ly	*nice* becomes *nicely*	tells how something is done
the noun ending -es	*dish* becomes *dishes*	shows more than one or plurals
the verb ending -ed	*kick* becomes *kicked* *bag* becomes *bagged*	shows action in the past
the suffixes -er and -or	*learn* becomes *learner* *direct* becomes *director*	shows one who does or is something

A. Change each of the words below according to the directions given. Write the new word on the blank provided.

	Word	Directions	New Word
1.	beach	make it more than one, or plural	_____
2.	loud	make it describe how someone talks	_____
3.	inspect	make it a person who does this	_____
4.	race	make it show the action of a fast car	_____
5.	read	make it a person who does this	_____
6.	wait	make it an action that happened in the past	_____
7.	toy	make it more than one, or plural	_____
8.	burn	make it show the action of a match	_____
9.	quick	make it describe how a mouse runs	_____
10.	box	make it more than one, or plural	_____
11.	dance	make it a person who does this	_____
12.	lunch	make it more than one, or plural	_____

Unit 2, Test

Part A: Antonyms

Directions: Choose the word that means about the opposite as the <u>underlined</u> word.

1. <u>dry</u> flowers
   - ○ pretty
   - ○ ugly
   - ○ smelly
   - ○ moist

2. to <u>whisper</u>
   - ○ shout
   - ○ listen
   - ○ run
   - ○ play

3. a <u>tardy</u> student
   - ○ cold
   - ○ long
   - ○ early
   - ○ wild

4. She will <u>obey</u>.
   - ○ laugh
   - ○ revolt
   - ○ stop
   - ○ start

5. a <u>fertile</u> field
   - ○ barren
   - ○ lush
   - ○ lovely
   - ○ full

6. a <u>bright</u> light
   - ○ model
   - ○ old
   - ○ dim
   - ○ neon

7. an <u>adolescent</u>
   - ○ boy
   - ○ child
   - ○ kid
   - ○ adult

8. <u>danger</u> ahead
   - ○ water
   - ○ safety
   - ○ wonder
   - ○ lessons

9. Sheila was a <u>genius</u>.
   - ○ dummy
   - ○ teen
   - ○ cheerleader
   - ○ wonder

10. <u>imperfect</u> work
    - ○ bad
    - ○ old
    - ○ excellent
    - ○ late

Unit 2, Test

Part B: Homophones

Directions: Fill in the circle next to the letter of the word that is a homophone of the **bold** word

1. **red**
   - Ⓐ rid
   - Ⓑ right
   - Ⓒ read
   - Ⓓ raise
   - Ⓔ real

2. **brake**
   - Ⓕ brack
   - Ⓖ back
   - Ⓗ brek
   - Ⓘ break
   - Ⓙ braik

3. **flu**
   - Ⓚ flute
   - Ⓛ foot
   - Ⓜ from
   - Ⓝ flood
   - Ⓞ flew

4. **knead**
   - Ⓟ need
   - Ⓠ knot
   - Ⓡ neat
   - Ⓢ knight
   - Ⓣ kneel

5. **medal**
   - Ⓐ meal
   - Ⓑ medic
   - Ⓒ maple
   - Ⓓ metal
   - Ⓔ mitten

6. **road**
   - Ⓕ rod
   - Ⓖ rowed
   - Ⓗ right
   - Ⓘ rose
   - Ⓙ roll

7. **heal**
   - Ⓚ heel
   - Ⓛ heed
   - Ⓜ heat
   - Ⓝ hill
   - Ⓞ hilt

8. **thrown**
   - Ⓟ throw
   - Ⓠ throne
   - Ⓡ through
   - Ⓢ troop
   - Ⓣ true

9. **wheel**
   - Ⓐ wheat
   - Ⓑ weed
   - Ⓒ well
   - Ⓓ wail
   - Ⓔ we'll

10. **horse**
    - Ⓕ hour
    - Ⓖ hors
    - Ⓗ hoarse
    - Ⓘ hers
    - Ⓙ hears

Unit 2, Test

Part C: Structural Analysis

Directions: Add an ending to each of the **bold** words below. The endings you will add are *s, es, ing, ly, ed, er,* and *or*. The directions will tell you how to change each **bold** word. Write your answer on the line provided.

1. Make the word **door** plural, or more than one. _____

2. Make the word **quick** tell how something falls. _____

3. Make the word **ride** show on-going action. _____

4. Make the verb **walk** show action in the past. _____

5. Make the word **teach** a person who instructs. _____

6. Make the word **beach** plural, or more than one. _____

7. Make the word **vertical** tell how someone climbed. _____

8. Make the verb **miss** show action in the past. _____

9. Make the word **roar** show on-going action. _____

10. Make the word **dance** a person who dances. _____

11. Make the word **canyon** plural, or more than one. _____

12. Make the word **urgent** tell how one needs help. _____

13. Make the word **inspect** a person who inspects. _____

14. Make the word **lunch** plural, or more than one. _____

15. Make the word **slide** show on-going action. _____

16. Make the verb **cash** show action in the past. _____

17. Make the word **loud** tell how someone yells. _____

18. Make the word **burn** show on-going action. _____

19. Make the word **box** plural, or more than one. _____

20. Make the word **brush** plural, or more than one. _____

Unit 3, Lesson 1

Power Words

Look at the words below. Circle any that you think you may know. Be ready to tell the class what the word means. Also tell the class how you think you know that word.

boatload	explode	increase	smokestack
crater	explore	information	spurting
erupt	frightens	shipwreck	thrill

Part 1: Compound Words

A **compound word** is a word made by putting two words together. Knowing the meaning of the smaller words helps you figure out the meaning of the whole word. For example, **lifeboat** is made up of the smaller words **life** and **boat**—a boat that saves lives. The word **waterfall** is made up of the smaller words **water** and **fall**—water that falls from a higher place to a lower place.

A. Combine these pairs of words to make compound words. Write the compound word on the lines.

1. smoke + stack = _____

2. dock + hand = _____

3. sea + shore = _____

4. sail + boat = _____

5. ship + wreck = _____

6. boat + load = _____

B. Use a compound word from Exercise A to complete each sentence.

1. The wind blew our _____ far out to sea.

2. The long pipe, or _____, sends the ashes into the air.

3. We could see the sinking ship from our house on the _____.

4. The divers found a _____ on the ocean floor.

5. The young _____ helped tie the boat to the dock.

6. The large ship was filled with a _____ of people.

Unit 3, Lesson 1

Part 2: Context Clues

When you come to a word that you don't know, look for words near the unknown word. These words may give you **context clues** that help you figure out what the unknown word means. One type of context clue is a **definition clue**. This type of clue tells the exact meaning of an unknown word. For example, in the sentence below the context clue tells you that the definition of *orbits* is "moves around."

The earth *orbits*, that is, it moves around the sun.

A. Look for definition clues. Write the definition of each **boldfaced** word on the line.

1. The **crater**, or hole at the top of the volcano, can be very large and deep.

   A **crater** is _____

2. The lady on the mountain was a **volcanologist**. She studied volcanoes.

   A **volcanologist** is _____

3. The hot rock flows up the **conduit**, which is the tube from the center of the volcano to the crater.

   The **conduit** is_____

4. The rock was **molten**. In other words, it turned into a liquid from intense heat.

   Molten means_____

5. Most of town was **incinerated** by the lava, that is, it was burned up.

   Incinerated means _____

B. Look up each word below in a dictionary if you do not know its meaning. Then, write a sentence using the word. In the sentence, provide a definition clue.

spurting _____

_____

fiery _____

_____

erupt_____

_____

Unit 3, Lesson 1

Part 3: Synonyms

A **synonym** is a word that has almost the same meaning as another word. For example, *strong* and *powerful* have almost the same meaning.

A. Darken the circle for the word from the list that is a synonym of the **boldfaced** word.

1. He would be taking a **risk** if he flew an old plane into a strong hurricane.
   - ○ wallet
   - ○ chance
   - ○ lie
   - ○ job

2. The rain was **striking** the window so hard it sounded like a drum.
   - ○ wetting
   - ○ falling
   - ○ filling
   - ○ beating

3. The weathermen gather **information** about the hurricane, such as its wind speed.
   - ○ facts
   - ○ drops
   - ○ plays
   - ○ flights

4. The pilots are so brave that very little **frightens** them.
   - ○ tells
   - ○ picks
   - ○ scares
   - ○ feeds

5. A hurricane is a powerful **tempest** with much rain and high winds.
   - ○ plane
   - ○ tree
   - ○ person
   - ○ storm

B. Each of the **bold** words below has a synonym that begins in the prefix "ex." Draw a line from the bold word to its synonym. If you need help, look the words up in a dictionary or thesaurus.

thrill	explode
burst	explore
search	exchange
increase	expand
trade	excite

Unit 3, Lesson 2

Power Words

Look at the words below. Circle any that you think you may know. Be ready to tell the class what the word means. Also tell the class how you think you know that word.

currency	iceberg	menace	underground
disaster	journey	outing	vessel
flood	malfunction	profit	watertight

Part 1: Compound Words

A **compound word** is a word made by putting two words together. Knowing the meaning of the smaller words helps you figure out the meaning of the whole word. For example, **motorcycle** is made up of the base words **motor** and **cycle**—a type of cycle powered by a motor.

A. Complete the chart below by breaking each compound word into its base words. Then write the meaning of the compound word, using a dictionary if needed. Finally, complete the sentences using the correct word from the chart.

Compound Word	Base Words	Meaning
sunlight		
weekend		
fireworks		
underground		
watertight		
withstand		
seamen		

1. Lava is melted rock that is deep _____.

2. The ship sank despite the _____ doors.

3. No one can _____ the force of a terrible hurricane.

4. In the middle of the hurricane, one flies through the clouds into _____.

5. Magma explodes out of the top of a volcano like _____.

Unit 3, Lesson 2

Part 2: Context Clues

Remember that **context clues** help you figure out what an unknown word means. One type of context clue is a **definition clue**. This type of clue tells the exact meaning of an unknown word. A **restatement clue** gives a synonym, or word with nearly the same meaning as the unknown word. For example, in the sentence below the restatement clue tells you that the synonym of *vessel* is "ship."

> The *vessel*, or ship, could carry thousands of people across the ocean.

A. Look for definition or restatement clues. Write the definition of each **boldfaced** word on the line. Use a dictionary if necessary.

1. The **meteorologist**, or weatherman, can tell you when a storm is coming.

   A **meteorolgist** is_____.

2. The *Titanic* hit an **iceberg**, or large body of floating ice.

   An **iceberg** is _____.

3. Volcanic eruptions often cause earthquakes, or **temblors**.

   The **temblor** is _____.

4. Hurricanes cause so much rain that floods, or **deluges**, are common.

   Deluge means _____.

5. There was a giant eruption of lava, or **discharge**, from Mt. St. Helens.

   Discharge means _____.

B. **Fluency:** Read the paragraph below. For each of the underlined words, write a synonym for that word above it. Use a dictionary or thesaurus if necessary.

The <u>seaman</u> had been on board the <u>vessel</u> for a long time. Their <u>journey</u> began

calmly. After three days, however, a great <u>storm</u> blew up. The <u>rain</u> came down so

hard that the captain was unable to <u>navigate</u>. The whole crew was <u>frightened</u>. They

knew they had taken a big <u>risk</u> by sailing out into a storm. They should have

gathered more <u>information</u> before leaving. It would have been a good idea to have

talked to a <u>meteorologist</u>. Next time the seaman would do things differently. If there

was a next time!

Unit 3, Lesson 2

Part 3: Synonyms

Remember that a **synonym** is a word that has almost the same meaning as another word. For example, *big* and *large* have almost the same meaning. They are synonyms.

A. Darken the circle for the word from the list that is a synonym of the **boldfaced** word.

1. Unable to find his keys, Paul **sought** for them in his room.
   - ○ spent
   - ○ searched
   - ○ sent
   - ○ played

2. Our car engine had a **malfunction**, and we stopped in the middle of the road.
   - ○ failure
   - ○ wish
   - ○ difference
   - ○ washing

3. Juanita used her **currency** to pay for gifts on her vacation.
   - ○ mother
   - ○ electricity
   - ○ house
   - ○ money

4. Jamie knew the mean dog was a real **menace**.
   - ○ dream
   - ○ boxer
   - ○ threat
   - ○ hungry

5. Businessmen hope they will **profit** from the things they sell.
   - ○ cry
   - ○ benefit
   - ○ sing
   - ○ lie

6. Every Sunday our family had an **outing** to our grandparents.
   - ○ car
   - ○ daydream
   - ○ trip
   - ○ argument

Unit 3, Lesson 3

Power Words Review

Look at the words below. Circle any that you think you may know. Be ready to tell the class what the word means. Also tell the class how you think you know that word.

boatload	explore	journey	smokestack
crater	flood	malfunction	spurting
currency	frighten	menace	thrill
disaster	iceberg	outing	underground
erupt	increase	profit	vessel
explode	information	shipwreck	watertight

Part 1: Compound Words

You remember that a **compound word** is a word made by putting two words together. Knowing the meaning of the smaller words helps you figure out the meaning of the whole word.

A. Look at the drawing below. Figure out where each of the following compound words is on the picture. Write the compound word in the correct blank by its object.

boatload	motorcycle	seashore	sunlight
dockhand	sailboat	shipwreck	
lifeboat	seaman	smokestack	

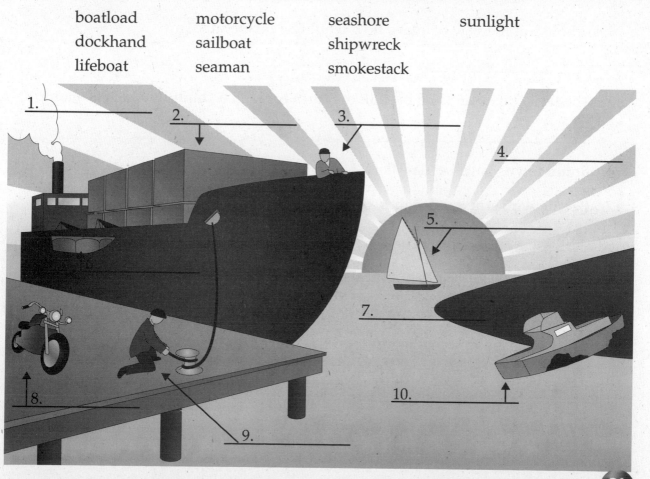

Unit 3, Lesson 3

Part 2: Context Clues

Remember that **context clues** help you figure out what an unknown word means. One type of context clue is a **definition clue**. This type of clue tells the exact meaning of an unknown word. A **restatement clue** gives a synonym, or word with nearly the same meaning as the unknown word.

A. In the blank provided, write a definition or restatement clue for the word or phrase in **bold**. Use a dictionary if necessary. Use the words below for your answers.

burned	explode	spurting	volcanologists
crater	melted	temblor	
disasters	meteorologists	tube	

1. Volcanoes can **erupt**, or _____, at any time.

2. Most of the lava comes out of the large **vent**, also known as the

    _____ in the top of the volcano.

3. Lava is also known as **molten**, or _____ rock.

4. A house in the way of a lava flow would be **incinerated**, or

    _____.

5. The lava comes up from deep in the earth through a **conduit**, which is a long

    _____

6. Entire towns have become fiery _____ or **ruins**.

7. **People who study volcanoes**, or _____, love to visit an active

    eruption.

8. A powerful eruption can cause an **earthquake**, also known as a

    _____.

9. Much ash can be seen **shooting**, or _____ into the sky.

10. This ash worries **weathermen**, or _____, because it can change the

    local weather.

Unit 3, Lesson 3

Part 3: Synonyms

A. Remember that a **synonym** is a word that has almost the same meaning as another word. The crossword puzzle uses words you've learned in the last two lessons. Use the clues at the bottom of the page to fill out the puzzle. Try to do the puzzle first. If you get stuck, then look back to Lessons 1 and 2 to find your answers. You may also look in a dictionary or thesaurus.

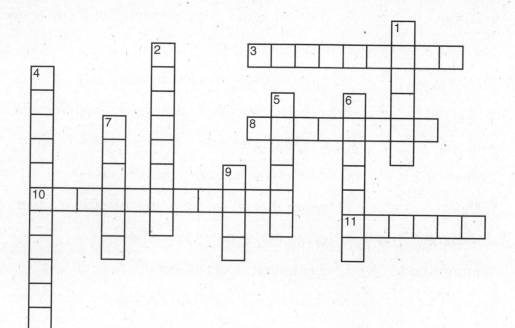

ACROSS:
3. scares
8. money
10. failure
11. searched

DOWN:
1. threat
2. beating
4. facts
5. trip
6. storm
7. benefit
9. chance

Unit 3, Test

Part A: Compound Words

Directions: Match the meaning of the compound word in **Column B** with the word in **Column A**. Fill in the letter of the definition on the blank provided.

Column A

1. _____ sunlight
2. _____ seashore
3. _____ boatload
4. _____ motorcycle
5. _____ withstand
6. _____ sailboat
7. _____ fireworks
8. _____ lifeboat
9. _____ dockhand
10. _____ underground
11. _____ seamen
12. _____ waterfall
13. _____ shipwreck
14. _____ weekend
15. _____ smokestack

Column B

A. sailors

B. the period of Friday through Sunday in a week

C. daylight

D. a boat that is powered by sails

E. a large funnel that takes smoke high into the air

F. the land where the ocean meets the beach

G. a two-wheeled, motor-driven cycle

H. water that falls from a high place to a lower one

I. cargo that is carried on a boat

J. a ship that is lost at sea

K. to stand with or up to pressure

L. a boat used to save lives on a sinking ship

M. under the surface of the earth

N. explosive devices which make noise and light

O. someone who works on a dock in a shipyard

Directions: Each of the following compound words has been divided into its base words in two ways. Only one choice is correct. Write the letter of the correct choice in the blank provided.

1. _____ shipwreck   A. ship / wreck   B. shi / pwreck

2. _____ underground   A. und / erground   B. under / ground

3. _____ seamen   A. sea / men   B. seam / en

4. _____ smokestack   A. smo / kestack   B. smoke / stack

Unit 3, Test

Part B: Context Clues

Directions: For each numbered blank, there is a list of words with the same number. Choose the word from each list that best completes the meaning of the paragraph.

1. The _____ moved in closer. Since she studied volcanoes, it was her job to
   (1)
   measure the size of the hole or _____ .
   (2)

1.		2.	
○	meteorologist	○	crater
○	volcanologist	○	tunnel
○	lava	○	tremor
○	tourist	○	den

2. One needs to be careful of the eruption or _____ from a volcano. This fire could
   (3)
   easily _____ anything.
   (4)

3.		4.	
○	water	○	wash away
○	outing	○	incinerate
○	sight	○	erupt
○	discharge	○	cook

3. The weatherman, or _____, was slow to warn people below the dam. He didn't
   (5)
   realize that the heavy rain had made a _____ .
   (6)

5.		6.	
○	volcanologist	○	iceberg
○	pilot	○	stream
○	meteorologist	○	deluge
○	captain	○	puddle

4. The rock had become _____. It was so hot that it had melted and was traveling
   (7)
   up the tube, or _____, to the top of the mountain.
   (8)

7.		8.	
○	soft	○	straw
○	molten	○	vessel
○	crater	○	conduit
○	brittle	○	gutter

Unit 3, Test

Part C: Synonyms

Directions: Fill in the letter of the word that is a synonym of the **bold** word.

1. gather **information**
   - Ⓐ plays
   - Ⓑ cards
   - Ⓒ facts
   - Ⓓ smells
   - Ⓔ flowers

2. a powerful **tempest**
   - Ⓕ scent
   - Ⓖ storm
   - Ⓗ wind
   - Ⓘ voice
   - Ⓙ athlete

3. a real **menace**
   - Ⓚ book
   - Ⓛ dream
   - Ⓜ wish
   - Ⓝ threat
   - Ⓞ fight

4. a family **outing**
   - Ⓟ trip
   - Ⓠ house
   - Ⓡ breakfast
   - Ⓢ doctor
   - Ⓣ argument

5. taking a **risk**
   - Ⓐ test
   - Ⓑ gift
   - Ⓒ letter
   - Ⓓ shot
   - Ⓔ chance

6. make a **profit**
   - Ⓕ deal
   - Ⓖ benefit
   - Ⓗ loss
   - Ⓘ lie
   - Ⓙ gamble

7. **striking** the window
   - Ⓚ lifting
   - Ⓛ opening
   - Ⓜ beating
   - Ⓝ breaking
   - Ⓞ cleaning

8. used her **currency**
   - Ⓟ time
   - Ⓠ money
   - Ⓡ mind
   - Ⓢ friend
   - Ⓣ car

9. it **frightens**
   - Ⓐ scares
   - Ⓑ speaks
   - Ⓒ leans
   - Ⓓ tries
   - Ⓔ dies

10. had a **malfunction**
    - Ⓕ party
    - Ⓖ blast
    - Ⓗ baby
    - Ⓘ failure
    - Ⓙ dinner

Unit 4, Lesson 1

Power Words

Look at the words below. Circle any that you think you may know. Be ready to tell the class what the word means. Also tell the class how you think you know that word.

autograph	dejectedly	hitchhike	offstage
biography	gesture	immigrant	periscope
biology	grammar	impress	photosensitive

Part 1: Compound Words

A **compound word** is a word made by putting two words together. Knowing the meaning of the smaller words helps you figure out the meaning of the whole word. For example, **outdoors** is made of the smaller words *out* and *doors*. You can figure out that outdoors means outside.

A. Combine each word in **Row 1** with a word in **Row 2** to make a compound word. Then write each compound word beside its definition below.

Row 1:   birth   hitch   news   earth   off

Row 2:   stage   man   quake   day   hike

1. a person who presents the news   _____

2. a trembling of the earth   _____

3. to catch a ride by walking along the road   _____

4. something that occurs off the main stage   _____

5. the day you are born   _____

B. Fluency: Practice reading the paragraph below until you can read it smoothly. Find and circle the five compound words from **Exercise A**.

Jose got the part of Manuel in the play. He had to pretend that the shoes he got for his birthday didn't fit properly. He told his friends offstage that he wasn't sure he liked the part. Mark got the part of Tio Jose, but he said he would never hitchhike to Modesto. It was too dangerous. Mark said that he heard a newsman tell about people who had been robbed while hitching a ride. Jose stomped the stage floor in the big shoes so hard it felt like an earthquake. He told Mark that no one would rob him in shoes as ugly as these.

Unit 4, Lesson 1

Part 2: Greek and Latin Roots

Many English words are made up of word parts from other languages, especially Greek and Latin. These word parts are called **roots**. A root cannot stand alone, but knowing its meaning helps you figure out the meaning of the whole word. A group of words with the same root is called a **word family**. Study the chart of **Greek** roots below.

Root	Meaning	Example
log	word, reason, study	geo<u>log</u>y
graph/gram	write, draw, describe	para<u>graph</u>
scope	see	tele<u>scope</u>
photo	light	<u>photo</u>graph
auto	self, alone	<u>auto</u>biography

A. Underline the root of each word in **Column A**. Then match each word with its correct meaning in **Column B**. Write the letter of the correct meaning in the space provided. Use a dictionary if necessary.

Column A

1. _____ photosensitive

2. _____ biography

3. _____ autoloading

4. _____ ecology

5. _____ geography

6. _____ photocopy

7. _____ biology

8. _____ grammar

9. _____ autograph

10. _____ periscope

Column B

A. the study of the environment

B. to sign one's name to something

C. a device to see objects from underwater

D. the science that describes the earth

E. a machine, such as a gun, that loads itself

F. to react or be sensitive to light

G. a description of someone's life

H. a description of how a language works

J. the study of living things

K. to use light to make a copy

Unit 4, Lesson 1

Part 3: Shades of Meaning

Words may have small differences in meaning. A reader must know the exact meaning of a word to understand what the writer is saying. For example, a boat that is *large* is different from a boat that is *huge*. Huge is much bigger than large.

A. Read the sentence with the missing word. Then read the question about the missing word. Choose the word that best answers the question.

1. Manuel wanted to _____ his friends at the party.

   Which of these words would indicate that Manuel wanted people to have a good opinion of him?

   A. talk to
   B. fight
   C. yell at
   D. impress

2. Tio Jose was a new _____ to the United States.

   Which of these words would indicate that Tio Jose just moved to America?

   A. friend
   B. immigrant
   C. relative
   D. neighbor

3. Tio Jose was touched by Manuel's _____ of giving him the shoes.

   Which of these words would indicate that Tio was touched by Manuel's action that showed his true feelings?

   A. habit
   B. game
   C. gesture
   D. excuse

4. Manuel walked back home _____ when he lost his money.

   Which of these words would indicate that Manuel was sad?

   A. quickly
   B. dejectedly
   C. freely
   D. hastily

Name _____ Date _____

Power Words

Look at the words below. Circle any that you think you may know. Be ready to tell the class what the word means. Also tell the class how you think you know that word.

accelerate	driftwood	outwit	slipknot
checkout	flexible	peeved	vision
deflect	hermit	scribe	vista

Part 1: Compound Words

Remember that a **compound word** is a word made by putting two words together. Knowing the meaning of the smaller words helps you figure out the whole word.

A. Circle the best way to break apart each **boldfaced** word so you can understand it. Then write a definition for the compound word on the line. Use a dictionary if needed.

1. My dad went down to the hotel lobby to **checkout**.

   a. chec-kout   b. check-out

   Checkout means: _____

2. Luis had difficulty with the **gearshift** when he was learning to drive.

   a. gear-shift   b. gears-hift

   Gearshift means: _____

3. My mom loves to collect **driftwood** along the beach.

   a. drift-wood   b. drif-twood

   Driftwood means: _____

4. The robber got away because he was tied down with a **slipknot**.

   a. sli-pknot   b. slip-knot

   Slipknot means: _____

5. With that storm coming, you better put on some **rainwear**.

   a. rainwe-ar   b. rain-wear

   Rainwear means: _____

Unit 4, Lesson 2

Part 2: Greek and Latin Roots

Many English words are made up of word parts from other languages, especially Greek and Latin. These word parts are called **roots**. A root cannot stand alone, but knowing its meaning helps you figure out the meaning of the whole word. A group of words with the same root is called a **word family**. Study the chart of **Latin** roots below.

Root	Meaning	Example
ject	throw, hurl	<u>ej</u>ect
vid/vis	see	<u>vid</u>eo
dic/dict	speak, say, tell	<u>dict</u>ionary
flect/flex	bend	re<u>flect</u>ion
scrib/script	write	pre<u>scrib</u>e

A. Underline the root of each word in **Column A**. Then match each word with its correct meaning in **Column B**. Write the letter of the correct meaning in the space provided. Use a dictionary if necessary.

Column A

1. _____ flexible

2. _____ vision

3. _____ project

4. _____ dictate

5. _____ scriptures

6. _____ deflect

7. _____ vista

8. _____ diction

9. _____ reflection

10. _____ scribe

Column B

A. to turn aside

B. able to be bent

C. use of words in speech or print

D. one who writes things down for others

E. to throw forward

F. to bounce back light from a surface

G. a distant view

H. eyesight, the ability to see

J. a sacred writing or book

K. to say aloud for another to write down

Unit 4, Lesson 2

Part 3: Shades of Meaning

Words may have small differences in meaning. A reader must know the exact meaning of a word to understand what the writer is saying. For example, a boat that is *large* is different from a boat that is *huge*. Huge is much bigger than large.

A. Read the sentence with the missing word. Then read the question about the missing word. Choose the word that best answers the question.

1. Sharon's new car will _____ quickly.

   Which of these words would indicate that Sharon's car will speed up quickly?

   A. sell
   B. fly
   C. accelerate
   D. turn

2. The smart fox was always able to _____ the hunting dogs.

   Which of these words would indicate that the fox is more clever than the dogs?

   A. outrun
   B. outwit
   C. escape
   D. hide from

3. John, the old _____, had been in that house since his family left.

   Which of these words would indicate that John is a person who lives alone and has little to do with others?

   A. hermit
   B. fool
   C. man
   D. grandfather

4. Manuel was really _____ that his shoes did not fit.

   Which of these words would indicate that Manuel was irritated?

   A. sad
   B. peeved
   C. happy
   D. injured

Unit 4, Lesson 3

Power Words Review

Look at the words below. Circle any that you think you may know. Be ready to tell the class what the word means. Also tell the class how you think you know that word.

accelerate	dejectedly	hitchhike	periscope
autograph	driftwood	immigrant	photosensitive
biography	flexible	impress	scribe
biology	gesture	offstage	slipknot
checkout	grammar	outwit	vision
deflect	hermit	peeved	vista

Part 1: Compound Words

A **compound word** is a word made by putting two words together. Knowing the meaning of the smaller words helps you figure out the meaning of the whole word.

A. The ten compound words below are hidden in this word search puzzle. Find each compound word and circle it. Words in the puzzle can be written across, up and down, backwards, or diagonally.

BIRTHDAY	GEARSHIFT	OFFSTAGE	NEWSMAN
CHECKOUT	HITCHHIKE	RAINWEAR	SLIPKNOT
DRIFTWOOD	EARTHQUAKE		

```
E  Y  S  M  V  L  H  P  H  D  J  J  S  F  A
R  A  A  X  I  Q  E  I  E  R  S  G  L  X  L
T  V  R  D  O  N  T  G  V  I  Y  J  I  Z  Y
H  K  S  T  H  C  A  I  T  F  L  P  P  Z  U
K  T  P  C  H  T  N  S  I  T  P  T  K  G  Z
F  S  U  H  S  Q  R  D  Q  W  S  U  N  M  M
F  U  I  F  U  D  U  I  W  O  F  O  O  O  W
S  K  F  X  C  S  B  A  B  O  G  K  T  J  N
E  O  D  V  L  U  Z  U  K  D  E  C  X  T  B
V  Y  T  F  I  H  S  R  A  E  G  E  C  A  F
N  A  M  S  W  E  N  C  W  M  E  H  W  A  Q
W  J  Z  S  Y  R  Z  J  H  S  S  C  U  P  I
J  Q  W  J  W  O  F  J  E  V  X  F  F  D  T
G  P  Y  R  A  I  N  W  E  A  R  T  J  Z  O
T  V  L  C  S  R  F  D  U  Z  Q  Z  G  C  J
```

Part 2: Greek and Latin Roots

Remember that many English words are made up of word parts from other languages, especially Greek and Latin. These word parts are called **roots**. Study the chart of roots.

Root	Meaning	Example
log	word, reason, study	geology
graph/gram	write, draw, describe	paragraph
scope	see	telescope
photo	light	photograph
auto	self, alone	autobiography
ject	throw, hurl	eject
vid/vis	see	video
dic/dict	speak, say, tell	dictionary
flect/flex	bend	reflection
scrib/script	write	prescribe

A. Match each word in **Column A** with its correct meaning in **Column B**. Write the letter of the correct meaning in the space provided. Use a dictionary if necessary.

Column A

1. _____ scribe
2. _____ biography
3. _____ autograph
4. _____ ecology
5. _____ geography
6. _____ vista
7. _____ periscope
8. _____ flexible

Column B

A. the study of the environment

B. one who writes things down for others

C. a device to see objects from underwater

D. the science that describes the earth

E. to sign one's name to something

F. able to be bent

G. a description of someone's life

H. a distant view

Part 3: Shades of Meaning

Words may have small differences in meaning. A reader must know the exact meaning of a word to understand what the writer is saying.

A. Read the sentence with the missing word. Then read the question about the missing word. Choose the word that best answers the question.

1. Kim's uncle was a new _____ to New Mexico.

   Which of these words would indicate that Kim's uncle just came to live in New Mexico?

   A. farmer
   B. neighbor
   C. tourist
   D. immigrant

2. The teacher was _____ at how badly her students did on the tests.

   Which of these words would indicate that the teacher was irritated?

   A. saddened
   B. peeved
   C. happy
   D. depressed

3. Coach Davis called a play to _____ the other team's coach.

   Which of these words would indicate that Coach Davis is more clever than the other team's coach?

   A. outwit
   B. tire
   C. stop
   D. irritate

4. Roberto left the field _____ when his team lost the game.

   Which of these words would indicate that Roberto was sad?

   A. quickly
   B. yelling
   C. freely
   D. dejectedly

Unit 4, Test

Part A: Compound Words

Directions: Match the meaning of the compound word in **Column B** with the word in **Column A**. Fill in the letter of the definition on the blank provided.

1. _____ checkout
2. _____ birthday
3. _____ newsman
4. _____ outdoors
5. _____ gearshift
6. _____ earthquake
7. _____ hitchhike
8. _____ slipknot
9. _____ rainwear
10. _____ offstage
11. _____ driftwood

A. a movement of the earth's surface

B. a knot that comes untied easily

C. to pay one's bill when leaving a hotel

D. the day on which someone is born

E. wood that floats on rivers or in the ocean

F. clothing worn in the rain

G. off the main stage in a dramatic production

H. outside

I. a lever for changing gears

J. to get a ride with a stranger by walking along the side of the road

K. someone who presents the news on TV or radio

Directions: Each of the following compound words has been divided into its base words in two ways. Only one choice is correct. Write the letter of the correct choice in the blank provided.

1. _____ offstage   A. of / fstage   B. off / stage

2. _____ slipknot   A. sli / pknot   B. slip / knot

3. _____ gearshift   A. gears / hift   B. gear / shift

4. _____ checkout   A. chec / kout   B. check / out

Unit 4, Test

Part B: Greek and Latin Roots

Directions: Match the meaning of the word in **Column B** with the word in **Column A**. Fill in the letter of the definition on the blank provided.

1. _____ vision   A. eyesight; the ability to see

2. _____ reflection   B. a device to see objects from underwater

3. _____ autoloading   C. a distant view

4. _____ periscope   D. use of words in speech or print

5. _____ biography   E. to sign one's name to something

6. _____ dictate   F. a sacred writing or book

7. _____ scriptures   G. able to be bent; bendable

8. _____ grammar   H. a description of someone's life

9. _____ diction   I.   the science that describes the earth

10. _____ flexible   J.   to throw or bend back light from a surface

11. _____ photosensitive   K. a description of how a language works

12. _____ deflect   L. a machine, such as a gun, that loads itself

13. _____ autograph   M. to say aloud things for another to write down

14. _____ geography   N. to turn something aside

15. _____ vista   O. to react or be sensitive to light

Directions: Each Latin and Greek root below has two definitions. Only one is correct. Write the letter of the correct one on the blank provided.

1. _____ photo   A. sound   B. light

2. _____ dic/dit   A. speak, say   B. to lead

3. _____ scope   A. far, distant   B. see

4. _____ graph/gram A. draw, describe   B. throw

Unit 4, Test

Part C: Shades of Meaning

Directions: Read the sentence with the missing word. Then read the question about the missing word. Choose the word that best answers the question.

1. Sarah was really _____ that she spilled ketchup on her white dress.

   Which of these words would indicate that Sarah was irritated?

   A. glad
   B. sad
   C. peeved
   D. injured

2. Jose walked home _____ the day he found out he didn't make the team.

   Which of these words would indicate that Jose was sad?

   A. dejectedly
   B. quickly
   C. wistfully
   D. hastily

3. Tom was able to _____ once his skateboard started down the hill.

   Which of these words would indicate that Tom sped up quickly?

   A. coast
   B. creep
   C. turn
   D. accelerate

4. Mr. Lee, our neighbor, is a new _____ to this country.

   Which of these words would indicate that Mr. Lee has just moved to this country?

   A. tourist
   B. salesman
   C. immigrant
   D. relative

5. My mom is always able to _____ us when we play games at home.

   Which of these words would indicate that mom is more clever than the others?

   A. outrun
   B. outdistance
   C. outpace
   D. outwit

Unit 5, Lesson 1

Power Words

Look at the words below. Circle any that you think you may know. Be ready to tell the class what the word means. Also tell the class how you think you know that word.

crossly	illiterate	inactive	reassure
disagree	impatiently	memories	recognize
disappear	improbable	misunderstand	wicked

Part 1: Prefixes and Base Words

A **base word** is a word that can stand alone. A **prefix** is a word part added to the beginning of a base word. For example, in the word **impossible**, *possible* is the base word and *im-* is the prefix added at the beginning. Knowing the meaning of a prefix helps you figure out the meaning of the whole word. *Impossible* means "not possible." Study the meaning of the following prefixes until you can remember what each means.

dis- means "not" or "lack of" / *mis-* means "wrong" or "wrongly"
im-, il-, and *in-* mean "not"

A. Draw a line between the base word and the prefix for each word below. Then write what the word means on the line. Use a dictionary if necessary.

1. inactive - _____

2. misread - _____

3. illegal - _____

4. disappear - _____

5. inoperative - _____

6. misunderstand - _____

7. improbable - _____

8. disagree - _____

9. illiterate - _____

10. mismanage - _____

11. inconsistent - _____

12. disarm - _____

Unit 5, Lesson 1

Part 2: Context Clues

Remember that you can often figure out the meaning of an unknown word from the words that appear nearby. The words or phrases that surround an unknown word are called **context clues**. For example, see how the words in the sentences below tell you that *depressed* means very sad.

> Jean was *depressed* over losing her dog. She cried all night long.

A. Use context clues to figure out the meaning of the **boldfaced** word. Darken in the circle with the correct definition.

1. Unhappy, Sachiko waited **impatiently** for her long-delayed Grandma.
   - ○ gladly
   - ○ angrily
   - ○ wisely
   - ○ nicely

2. She had a **wicked** idea and decided not to take care of her Grandma.
   - ○ bad; evil
   - ○ smart
   - ○ silly
   - ○ interesting

3. Sachiko's Grandma had a disease. It made it difficult for her to **recognize** the people she once knew.
   - ○ like
   - ○ talk to
   - ○ care about
   - ○ know

4. She answered her mother **crossly** when she didn't want to do what she was told.
   - ○ in a sweet way
   - ○ in a nice way
   - ○ in a bored way
   - ○ in an angry way

5. Sachiko had to **reassure** her Grandma when she became frightened.
   - ○ feed
   - ○ dress
   - ○ calm
   - ○ walk

6. It was sad to Sachiko that her Grandma had lost her **memories**.
   - ○ children
   - ○ recollections
   - ○ attitude
   - ○ wealth

Unit 5, Lesson 1

Part 3: Syllabication

A **syllable** is a word part with one vowel sound. Remember that the vowels are the letters *a, e, i, o, u,* and sometimes *y.* All other letters are consonants. The chart below shows you the long and short vowel sounds.

Vowel	Long Sound	Short Sound
a	"a" as in day	"a" as in cat
e	"e" as in be	"e" as in set
i	"i" as in lie	"i" as in sit
o	"o" as in low	"o" as in hot
u	"u" as in blue	"u" as in bug

If you break an unknown word into syllables, it may help you figure out what the word means. Look at the rules below to see the correct places to divide words into syllables.

1. *war • plane* (between two words of a compound word)
2. *dis • arm* or *try • ing* (between a base word and a prefix or suffix)
3. *cor • rect* (between double consonants)
4. *clus • ter* (between two consonants, with vowels both before and after)
5. *be • hind* (<u>before</u> a single consonant if the vowel before it has a <u>long</u> sound)
6. *nev • er* (<u>after</u> a single consonant if the vowel before it has a <u>short</u> sound)

A. Use the rules above to divide each of the words below into its syllables. Write the syllables on the blanks provided. Then write which rule tells you how to divide a word.

Word	Syllables		Rule
1. crossly	= _____	+ _____	_____
2. summer	= _____	+ _____	_____
3. misread	= _____	+ _____	_____
4. profit	= _____	+ _____	_____
5. upstairs	= _____	+ _____	_____
6. window	= _____	+ _____	_____
7. wider	= _____	+ _____	_____
8. magic	= _____	+ _____	_____
9. fencepost	= _____	+ _____	_____
10. snuggle	= _____	+ _____	_____

Unit 5, Lesson 2

Power Words

Look at the words below. Circle any that you think you may know. Be ready to tell the class what the word means. Also tell the class how you think you know that word.

amazement	dispatched	inspection	qualify
boulevard	grandest	marathon	silliest
braced	grieve	participation	temptation

Part 1: Suffixes and Base Words

A **base word** is a word that can stand alone. A **suffix** is a word part added to the end of a base word. For example, in the word **sicker,** *sick* is the base word and *-er* is the suffix added at the end. Knowing the meaning of a suffix helps you figure out the meaning of the whole word. *Sicker* means "more sick." Study the meaning of the following suffixes until you can remember what each means.

-er means "more" / *-est* means "the most"
-ation, -ion, -sion, and *-ment* mean "a state or quality of"

A. Draw a line between the base word and the suffix for each word below. Then write what the word means on the line. Use a dictionary if necessary.

1. louder - _____

2. temptation - _____

3. amazement - _____

4. grandest - _____

5. participation - _____

6. weaker - _____

7. wonderment - _____

8. silliest - _____

9. recognition - _____

10. encouragement - _____

11. inspection - _____

12. amusement - _____

Unit 5, Lesson 2

Part 2: Context Clues

Remember that you can often figure out the meaning of an unknown word from the words that appear nearby. The words or phrases that surround an unknown word are called **context clues**. For example, see how the words in the sentences below tell you that *fatigued* means very tired.

Jean was *fatigued* after the long run. She was so tired she took a nap.

A. Use context clues to figure out the meaning of the **boldfaced** word. Darken in the circle with the correct definition.

1. Eduardo entered a **marathon** that was twenty-six miles long.
   - ○ contest
   - ○ competition
   - ○ game
   - ○ race

2. To **qualify** for the team, you must be very fast and in good shape.
   - ○ make a show
   - ○ practice
   - ○ fit the requirements
   - ○ lose your place

4. Sean walked down the tree-lined **boulevard** looking at the cars.
   - ○ raceway
   - ○ wide street
   - ○ pathway
   - ○ sidewalk

2. I will **grieve** when my old cat dies.
   - ○ sing
   - ○ be quiet
   - ○ feel sorrow
   - ○ be scared

5. The police car was **dispatched** to the scene of the accident.
   - ○ sent off
   - ○ shot
   - ○ wired
   - ○ led

6. The building was **braced** against the high wind.
   - ○ slanted
   - ○ welded
   - ○ made steady
   - ○ decorated

Unit 5, Lesson 2

Part 3: Syllabication

A **syllable** is a word part with one vowel sound. If you break an unknown word into syllables, it may help you figure out what the word means. Look at the rules below to see the correct places to divide words into syllables. Remember that the vowels are the letters *a, e, i, o, u,* and sometimes *y*. All other letters are consonants.

1. *war • plane* (between two words of a compound word)
2. *dis • arm* or *quick • ly* (between a base word and a prefix or suffix)
3. *cor • rect* (between double consonants)
4. *clus • ter* (between two consonants, with vowels both before and after)
5. *de • cide* (<u>before</u> a single consonant if the vowel before it has a <u>long</u> sound)
6. *nev • er* (<u>after</u> a single consonant if the vowel before it has a <u>short</u> sound)

A. Write the syllables of the words below on the lines. Then on the third blank provided, write the number of the rule from above that tells you how to separate each word.

		Syllables	**Rule**
1. grandest	_____ +	_____	_____
2. dresser	_____ +	_____	_____
3. photo	_____ +	_____	_____
4. girlfriend	_____ +	_____	_____
5. model	_____ +	_____	_____
6. dispatch	_____ +	_____	_____
7. jacket	_____ +	_____	_____
8. before	_____ +	_____	_____
9. dinner	_____ +	_____	_____
10. inside	_____ +	_____	_____
11. weaker	_____ +	_____	_____
12. second	_____ +	_____	_____

Unit 5, Lesson 3

Power Words Review

Look at the words below. Circle any that you think you may know. Be ready to tell the class what the word means. Try to use the word in a sentence to show its meaning.

amazement	dispatched	inactive	qualify
boulevard	grandest	inspection	reassure
braced	grieve	marathon	recognize
crossly	illiterate	memories	silliest
disagree	impatiently	misunderstand	temptation
disappear	improbable	participation	wicked

Part 1: Affixes and Base Words

Remember that a **base word** is a word that can stand alone. An **affix** is a word part added to the beginning or end of a base word. **Prefixes** and **suffixes** are affixes. Study the meaning of the following prefixes until you can remember what each means.

dis- means "not" or "lack of" / **mis-** means "wrong" or "wrongly"
im-, il-, and **in-** mean "not"
-er means "more" / **-est** means "the most"
-ation, -ion, -sion, and **-ment** mean "a state or quality of"

A. Match the word in **Column A** with its correct definition in **Column B**. Write the letter of the correct definition in the blank. Use a dictionary if necessary.

Column A

1. _____ inactive
2. _____ silliest
3. _____ illiterate
4. _____ disappear
5. _____ improbable
6. _____ misunderstand
7. _____ amazement
8. _____ temptation
9. _____ disagree
10. _____ participation

Column B

A. in a state of being amazed or impressed

B. not likely to happen; not probable

C. not to agree with someone

D. the most funny or foolish

E. not to understand or comprehend

F. the state of taking part or joining in

G. the state of being tempted or provoked

H. not able to read; not literate

I. to vanish or go away

J. not active

Unit 5, Lesson 3

Part 2: Context Clues

Remember that you can often figure out the meaning of an unknown word from the words that appear nearby. The words or phrases that surround an unknown word are called **context clues**.

A. Use context clues to figure out the meaning of the **boldfaced** word. Darken in the circle with the correct definition.

1. Terri had to know how to shoot well to **qualify** for the free throw contest.
   - ○ run for
   - ○ fit the requirements
   - ○ practice
   - ○ win

2. The thief was a **wicked** person. He would only steal from the old.
   - ○ lazy
   - ○ silly
   - ○ bad; evil
   - ○ interesting

4. The people in the fishing village will **grieve** for the sailors lost in the storm.
   - ○ speak
   - ○ feel sorrow
   - ○ care
   - ○ sing

2. The driver answered the policeman **crossly** when she was accused of speeding.
   - ○ in a sweet way
   - ○ in a tough way
   - ○ in a bored way
   - ○ in an angry way

5. An ambulance was **dispatched** to the accident on Central Avenue.
   - ○ sent off
   - ○ lost
   - ○ led
   - ○ flown

6. We have such wonderful **memories** of our fun days at the beach.
   - ○ dreams
   - ○ recollections
   - ○ attitudes
   - ○ photos

Unit 5, Lesson 3

Part 3: Syllabication

Syllables are word parts with one vowel sound each. Remember that prefixes and suffixes are usually separate word parts. Divide words into syllables between double consonants. If necessary, look up words in a dictionary to separate them into syllables.

A. Separate the following words into syllables. Write the syllables on the lines.

1. disarm = _____ + _____

2. grandest = _____ + _____

3. summer = _____ + _____

4. jacket = _____ + _____

5. girlfriend = _____ + _____

6. magic = _____ + _____

7. dispatch = _____ + _____

8. disappear = _____ + _____ + _____

9. reassure = _____ + _____ + _____

10. illegal = _____ + _____ + _____

B. Fluency: Practice reading the following story until you can read it smoothly. For each underlined word, write the number of syllables that word has in the blank. Remember that a syllable is a word part with <u>one</u> vowel sound. Use a dictionary if necessary.

The people in the company became <u>sadder</u> _____ every day. Their boss seemed to <u>mismanage</u> _____ most of the business. He came up with the <u>grandest</u> _____ ideas. He would <u>reassure</u> _____ all the employees that his ideas would work. However, everything he did made the company <u>weaker</u> _____. The boss didn't do anything <u>illegal</u> _____ or <u>wicked</u> _____, he just could not <u>recognize</u> _____ the right things to do to make the company better.

One day, however, while the boss was walking down the <u>boulevard</u> _____, he got a new idea. He rushed back to the office, and after a quick <u>inspection</u> _____, he knew his idea would work. To the <u>amazement</u> _____ of his employees, it did. The company was saved.

Unit 5, Test

Part A: Prefixes and Suffixes

Directions: Fill in the letter of the word that most nearly matches the meaning of the underlined word.

1. It's <u>illegal</u>.
   - Ⓐ interesting
   - Ⓑ unsatisfactory
   - Ⓒ truthful
   - Ⓓ unfair
   - Ⓔ unlawful

2. her <u>temptation</u>
   - Ⓕ desire
   - Ⓖ lawyer
   - Ⓗ imagination
   - Ⓘ ideas
   - Ⓙ wish

3. <u>mismanage</u> the job
   - Ⓚ sell
   - Ⓛ quit
   - Ⓜ ruin
   - Ⓝ make
   - Ⓞ succeed at

4. with <u>amazement</u>
   - Ⓟ sorrow
   - Ⓠ pay
   - Ⓡ weight
   - Ⓢ wonder
   - Ⓣ tragedy

5. to <u>disappear</u>
   - Ⓐ stop
   - Ⓑ vanish
   - Ⓒ play
   - Ⓓ go
   - Ⓔ appear

6. an <u>inactive</u> teammate
   - Ⓕ unfaithful
   - Ⓖ silly
   - Ⓗ awkward
   - Ⓘ lazy
   - Ⓙ cowardly

7. an <u>inoperative</u> engine
   - Ⓚ old
   - Ⓛ broken
   - Ⓜ fixed
   - Ⓝ well-running
   - Ⓞ fast

8. the <u>grandest</u> speech
   - Ⓟ most boring
   - Ⓠ longest
   - Ⓡ most wonderful
   - Ⓢ silliest
   - Ⓣ most hateful

9. the <u>silliest</u> joke
   - Ⓐ stupidest
   - Ⓑ warmest
   - Ⓒ nicest
   - Ⓓ worse
   - Ⓔ best

10. with <u>encouragement</u>
    - Ⓕ safety
    - Ⓖ purpose
    - Ⓗ support
    - Ⓘ ruin
    - Ⓙ bravery

Unit 5, Test

Part B: Context Clues

Directions: For each numbered blank, there is a list of words with the same number. Choose the word from each list that best completes the meaning of the paragraph.

1. My brother will _____. He will also have many fond _____ of our dead
   (1)   (2)
   grandmother to remember.

   1. ○ disagree   2. ○ tokens
       ○ laugh   ○ memories
       ○ leave   ○ photos
       ○ grieve   ○ reassures

2. The sign needs to be _____. If it isn't there is a chance a high wind could blow it
   (3)
   across the wide _____ where it would hit a car.
   (4)

   3. ○ braced   4. ○ marathon
       ○ made   ○ sidewalk
       ○ dispatched   ○ boulevard
       ○ wide   ○ desert

3. Jamie is _____. He tells lies about everyone; he steals things and he hurts his
   (5)
   friends' feelings by answering them _____.
   (6)

   5. ○ crossly   6. ○ crossly
       ○ welcome   ○ sweetly
       ○ wicked   ○ wicked
       ○ wise   ○ honestly

4. Larry entered a _____. He practiced for weeks to _____ for the race.
   (7)   (8)
   7. ○ boulevard   8. ○ recognize
       ○ raffle   ○ sneak into
       ○ marathon   ○ qualify
       ○ game   ○ sing

Unit 5, Test

Part C: Syllabication

Directions: Separate the following words into syllables. Write the syllables on the lines.

1. sadder   = _____ + _____

2. dispatch   = _____ + _____

3. magic   = _____ + _____

4. girlfriend   = _____ + _____

5. amazement   = _____ + _____ + _____

6. weaker   = _____ + _____

7. inspection   = _____ + _____ + _____

8. amusement   = _____ + _____ + _____

9. grandest   = _____ + _____

10. jacket   = _____ + _____

11. misread   = _____ + _____

12. disarm   = _____ + _____

13. illegal   = _____ + _____ + _____

14. mismanage   = _____ + _____ + _____

15. inactive   = _____ + _____ + _____

16. disagree   = _____ + _____ + _____

17. disappear   = _____ + _____ + _____

18. wicked   = _____ + _____

19. reassure   = _____ + _____ + _____

20. summer   = _____ + _____

Unit 6, Lesson 1

Power Words

Look at the words below. Circle any that you think you may know. Be ready to tell the class what the word means. Also tell the class how you think you know that word.

box	distract	jabbering	preference
check	envy	marble	watered
coat	expression	personal	whirled

Part 1: Idioms

An **idiom** is a statement or phrase that doesn't mean exactly what the words say. People in different places have different ways of saying things. For example, to say that a person "has a green thumb" does not mean that his thumb is the color green. It means that this person is able to grow plants very easily. "Has a green thumb" is an idiom.

A. Each sentence below has an underlined idiom. Use the words around the idiom to help you figure out what the idiom means. Then read the list of definitions below. Write the letter of the definition that matches the idiom in the line behind the sentence.

A. feeling great
B. lose control; get very mad
C. very jealous
D. got very tired
E. not smile or laugh

F. very clumsy
G. fail to follow through or finish
H. think seriously or plan
I. to be exactly right
J. to be mistaken or wrong

1. Tom made a mess while painting. He was <u>all thumbs</u> with a paintbrush. _____

2. He knew he couldn't <u>drop the ball</u> though. He had to get the job done. _____

3. If Aunt Polly saw him not painting, she would really <u>fly off the handle</u>. _____

4. Jim would not help. He told Tom that he was <u>barking up the wrong tree</u>. _____

5. Tom thought of a way to get help painting. He <u>put on his thinking cap</u>. _____

6. When he began to fool others, he knew he had <u>hit the nail on the head</u>. _____

7. The other boys were all <u>green with envy</u> that Tom had such a great job. _____

8. As each boy <u>ran out of gas</u>, Tom convinced another to start painting. _____

9. It was hard for Tom to <u>keep a straight face</u> as the boys did all the work. _____

10. When the fence was finished, Tom felt like he was <u>walking on air</u>. _____

Unit 6, Lesson 1

Part 2: Synonyms

Words that have nearly the same meaning are called **synonyms**. For example, **merry** and **happy** both mean about the same thing. These two words are synonyms.

A. Darken the circle for the word from the list that is a synonym of the **boldfaced** word in the sentence. Use the ideas in the sentence to help you decide.

1. Pat felt that a toothbrush is a very **personal** thing.
   - ○ silly
   - ○ wonderful
   - ○ stupid
   - ○ private

2. The **expression** on Violet's face never changed as Pat tried to make up his mind.
   - ○ look
   - ○ scar
   - ○ food
   - ○ shock

3. Violet tried to **distract** Pat while he was making his decision.
   - ○ kill
   - ○ disturb
   - ○ beat
   - ○ catch

4. Violet said she didn't have a **preference** as to which one she wanted.
   - ○ liking
   - ○ choice
   - ○ system
   - ○ idea

5. Violet kept **jabbering** at Pat to keep him confused so that he couldn't decide.
   - ○ punching
   - ○ kicking
   - ○ talking
   - ○ singing

6. Pat got mad at Violet and **whirled** around on her, telling her to go away.
   - ○ spun
   - ○ ran
   - ○ walked
   - ○ twisted

Unit 6, Lesson 1

Part 3: Multiple-Meaning Words

The word *multiple* means many. **Multiple-meaning words** are words that have more than one meaning. For example, the word *fly* can mean to sail through the air. It can also be a type of insect.

A. Read each sentence below. Think about how the **boldfaced** word in the sentence is used. Then read the different meanings of that word below. Write the letter of the definition in the blank that matches the meaning of the boldfaced word in the sentence.

_____ 1. Tom told his friends that painting **suits** him.
    a. clothing that consist of pants and a jacket
    b. pleases

_____ 2. Each of the boys **touched** the fence with the paintbrush by the end of the day.
    a. to make physical contact with
    b. to affect someone's emotions

_____ 3. Tom sat on a wooden **box** as the boys painted the fence for him.
    a. a container with four sides, a base and a cover
    b. to hit with the hand or fist

_____ 4. Tom's description of painting put the job in a new **light**.
    a. something of very little weight
    b. a source of illumination, such as a lamp
    c. a way of looking at something

_____ 5. Tom stepped back to **check** the work of the other painters.
    a. a sudden stop
    b. to inspect or look at closely
    c. a bill at a restaurant

_____ 6. His mouth **watered** at the sight of the delicious apple.
    a. to deliver water or another liquid to something
    b. to create saliva in the mouth in anticipation of eating food

_____ 7. One boy offered Tom the toys and a **marble** from his pocket.
    a. a type of rock used in buildings and sculpture
    b. a small glass ball used in children's games

_____ 8. By the end of the day, the fence had a fresh **coat** of paint on it.
    a. a piece of clothing with sleeves that is worn over other clothing
    b. a layer of material covering something

Unit 6, Lesson 2

Power Words

Look at the words below. Circle any that you think you may know. Be ready to tell the class what the word means. Also tell the class how you think you know that word.

block	distinct	narrative	snarled
chaos	fast	pampered	stole
court	mine	proprietor	store

Part 1: Idioms

Remember that an **idiom** is a statement or phrase that doesn't mean exactly what the words say. For example, to say that a person is "under the weather" does not mean that the person is standing in the rain. It means that the person is sick. "Under the weather" is an idiom.

A. Each sentence below has an underlined idiom. Use the words around the idiom to help you figure out what the idiom means. Then read the list of definitions below. Write the letter of the definition that matches the idiom in the line behind the sentence.

A. decide to do something
B. something very difficult
C. join in with everyone else
D. wasting time; not serious
E. not paying attention; lost in thought

F. mad about something in the past
G. get down to hard work
H. think seriously or plan
I. just about to say something
J. pay attention to

1. Violet was just <u>beating around the bush</u> when she was joking to Pat. _____

2. Pat had his decision on <u>the tip of his tongue</u> but didn't say it. _____

3. Aunt Polly told Tom to just <u>bite the bullet</u> and get started painting. _____

4. She wanted the kids <u>to get down to business</u> and make a decision. _____

5. It was like <u>pulling teeth</u> to get Tom to do any work. _____

6. Tom told everyone <u>to climb on the bandwagon</u> and help paint the fence. _____

7. Work to Tom meant he'd have <u>to put his nose to the grindstone</u>. _____

8. Pat had <u>a chip on his shoulder</u> when his sister told him to do anything. _____

9. Normally Violet wouldn't <u>give</u> Pat <u>the time of day</u> when he was talking. _____

10. Tom never paid attention. He was always <u>out to lunch</u>. _____

Unit 6, Lesson 2

Part 2: Synonyms

Words that have nearly the same meaning are called **synonyms**. For example, **merry** and **happy** both mean about the same thing. These two words are synonyms.

A. Darken the circle for the word from the list that is a synonym of the **boldfaced** word in the sentence. Use the ideas in the sentence to help you decide.

1. Traffic was **snarled** on the freeway, and we were late.
   - ○ fast
   - ○ wonderful
   - ○ tangled
   - ○ light

2. The kids are so **pampered;** they have everything they want.
   - ○ cute
   - ○ spoiled
   - ○ lazy
   - ○ mean

3. Mr. Davis is the **proprietor** of the store and decides what to buy and sell.
   - ○ owner
   - ○ clerk
   - ○ janitor
   - ○ stock boy

4. The earthquake caused great **chaos** among the people who didn't know what to do.
   - ○ anger
   - ○ weeping
   - ○ damage
   - ○ confusion

5. Sammy told us an interesting **narrative** about a family on vacation.
   - ○ melody
   - ○ lie
   - ○ story
   - ○ joke

6. Jeff had a **distinct** idea of exactly how to finish the game.
   - ○ wild
   - ○ silly
   - ○ confusing
   - ○ clear

Unit 6, Lesson 2

Part 3: Multiple-Meaning Words

The word *multiple* means many. **Multiple-meaning words** are words that have more than one meaning. For example, the word *fast* can mean to move quickly. It can also mean to choose to go without food for a long period of time.

A. Read each sentence below. Think about how the **boldfaced** word in the sentence is used. Then read the different meanings of that word below. Write the letter of the definition in the blank that matches the meaning of the boldfaced word in the sentence.

_____ 1. The rich lady always wore her beautiful **stole** to the theater.
    a. past tense of the verb *steal*
    b. a long scarf or robe made of expensive material

_____ 2. The poor man was taken to **court** before the judge.
    a. an open area of ground partly enclosed by walls
    b. a place where people are judged
    c. to try to win someone's affection in order to marry him or her

_____ 3. The people did not want to leave their **land**.
    a. the solid ground of the earth
    b. a nation or country
    c. to come to shore or descend down to earth

_____ 4. The old man put up his hand to **show** the king that he had nothing to eat.
    a. to cause to be seen; to display
    b. a performance
    c. a radio or television program

_____ 5. The farmers will not **store** enough food for winter if it doesn't rain.
    a. a place where merchandise is sold
    b. to save up for future use

_____ 6. The boxer used his right fist to **block** his opponent.
    a. to stop
    b. a solid piece of hard substance
    c. a part of a neighborhood bound by four streets

_____ 7. The king brought out his lunch so I brought out **mine**.
    a. belonging to me
    b. an excavation or hole in the earth from which ore and minerals are dug

_____ 8. It took a lot of courage to **face** the king.
    a. the front of the head from the forehead to the chin
    b. to stand in front of with complete awareness

Unit 6, Lesson 3

Power Words Review

Look at the words below. Circle any that you think you may know. Be ready to tell the class what the word means. Try to use the word in a sentence to show its meaning.

block	distinct	marble	proprietor
box	distract	mine	snarled
chaos	envy	narrative	stole
check	expression	pampered	store
coat	fast	personal	watered
court	jabbering	preference	whirled

Part 1: Idioms

Remember that an **idiom** is a statement or phrase that doesn't mean exactly what the words say.

A. Match the idiom in **Column A** with its meaning in **Column B**. Write the letter of the correct definition in the blank provided.

Column A

1. _____ pulling teeth

2. _____ chip on his shoulder

3. _____ green with envy

4. _____ run out of gas

5. _____ give the time of day

6. _____ the tip of his tongue

7. _____ put on this thinking cap

8. _____ climb on the bandwagon

9. _____ hit the nail on the head

10. _____ all thumbs

11. _____ fly off the handle

12. _____ walking on air

Column B

A. feeling great

B. think seriously or plan

C. just about to say something

D. get something exactly right

E. very clumsy

F. get very mad

G. mad about something in the past

H. something very difficult

I. join in with everyone else

J. jealous

K. pay attention to

L. get very tired; run out of energy

Unit 6, Lesson 3

Part 2: Synonyms

A. Remember that a **synonym** is a word that has almost the same meaning as another word. The crossword puzzle uses words you've learned in the last two lessons. Use the clues at the bottom of the page to fill out the puzzle. Try to do the puzzle first. If you get stuck, look back to Lessons 1 and 2 to find your answers. You may also look in a dictionary or thesaurus.

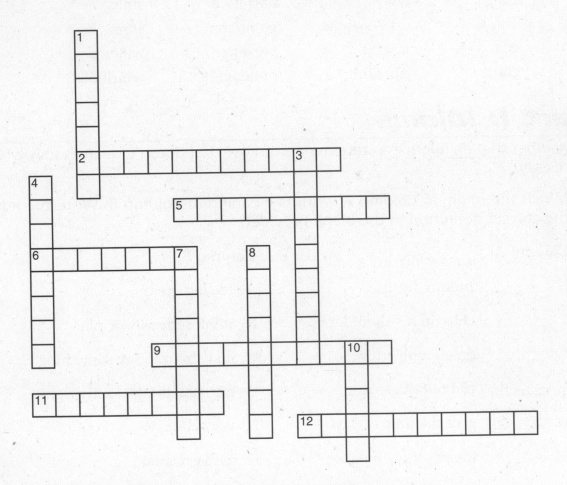

Across
2. look
5. talking
6. tangled
9. liking
11. clear
12. owner

Down
1. spun
3. story
4. private
7. disturb
8. spoiled
10. confusion

Unit 6, Lesson 3

Part 3: Multiple-Meaning Words

The word *multiple* means many. **Multiple-meaning words** are words that have more than one meaning.

A. Read each sentence below. Find the word that fits in both sentences.

1. Yolanda couldn't wait to open the large gift _____.

   Tom was learning to _____ in self-defense class.

   ○ package
   ○ hit
   ○ box
   ○ present

2. The columns in front of the building were made out of _____.

   Tom had a round green _____ that was his favorite toy.

   ○ glass
   ○ spaceship
   ○ wood
   ○ marble

3. Jose's mouth _____ every time he saw a pepperoni pizza.

   The gardener _____ the plants on hot, dry days.

   ○ watered
   ○ ached
   ○ fed
   ○ chopped

4. The teacher was _____ by the presents his class gave to him.

   David's dad _____ his son's shoulder to let him know he was behind him.

   ○ pleased
   ○ touched
   ○ hit
   ○ patted

5. Dad wrote a _____ to pay for the food.

   My mom will _____ in on us when we have a pajama party.

   ○ follow
   ○ look
   ○ check
   ○ make

Unit 6, Test

Part A: Idioms

Directions: Match the idiom in **Column A** with its meaning in **Column B**. Write the letter of the correct definition in the blank provided.

Column A

1. _____ fly off the handle

2. _____ bite the bullet

3. _____ hit the nail on the head

4. _____ pulling teeth

5. _____ green with envy

6. _____ nose to the grindstone

7. _____ all thumbs

8. _____ climb on the bandwagon

9. _____ put on his thinking cap

10. _____ walking on air

11. _____ the tip of his tongue

12. _____ chip on his shoulder

13. _____ give the time of day

14. _____ ran out of gas

15. _____ drop the ball

Column B

A. ran out of energy

B. feeling great

C. clumsy

D. to be exactly right

E. get very mad

F. to be very jealous

G. pay attention to

H. fail to follow through or finish

I. just about to say something

J. decide to do something

K. angry about something from the past

L. join in with everyone else

M. think seriously or plan

N. get down to hard work

O. something very difficult

Unit 6, Test

Part B: Synonyms

Directions: Choose the word that means about the same as the underlined word.

1. That's <u>personal</u>.
   - ○ mean
   - ○ silly
   - ○ tricky
   - ○ private

2. so <u>pampered</u>
   - ○ fresh
   - ○ old
   - ○ spoiled
   - ○ sad

3. a <u>narrative</u>
   - ○ poem
   - ○ article
   - ○ story
   - ○ watch

4. have a <u>preference</u>
   - ○ liking
   - ○ choice
   - ○ dinner
   - ○ way

5. a <u>distinct</u> idea
   - ○ nice
   - ○ terrible
   - ○ lovely
   - ○ clear

6. a silly <u>expression</u>
   - ○ look
   - ○ speech
   - ○ idea
   - ○ teacher

7. the <u>proprietor</u>
   - ○ store
   - ○ owner
   - ○ mailman
   - ○ producer

8. <u>snarled</u> traffic
   - ○ bad
   - ○ tangled
   - ○ wonderful
   - ○ fast

9. to <u>distract</u>
   - ○ disturb
   - ○ run
   - ○ speak
   - ○ question

10. <u>chaos</u> began
    - ○ teaching
    - ○ selling
    - ○ traveling
    - ○ confusion

Unit 6, Test

Part C: Multiple-Meaning Words

Directions: Read each sentence below. Find the word that fits in both sentences.

1. That hat is _____.

   Gold is dug out of a very deep _____ .

   ○ green
   ○ large
   ○ mine
   ○ hole

2. After winning the race, I saw Teri in a whole new _____.

   Rene is so thin she's as _____ as a feather.

   ○ way
   ○ slender
   ○ light
   ○ skinny

3. I couldn't _____ my dad when I got a speeding ticket.

   Sandy put a lot of makeup on her _____ .

   ○ face
   ○ see
   ○ love
   ○ skin

4. The mother was _____ when her children all came home for summer.

   Sam _____ his friend to let him know he was in the dark theater too.

   ○ spoke to
   ○ touched
   ○ taken
   ○ waved to

5. Many people move to a new _____ to find a better way to live.

   The bird will _____ on your shoulder if you hold still.

   ○ place
   ○ house
   ○ sit
   ○ land

Unit 7, Lesson 1

Power Words

Look at the words below. Circle any that you think you may know. Be ready to tell the class what the word means. Also tell the class how you think you know that word.

awkward	courses	finals	reflexes
cocky	dazed	goggles	relay
contract	depressed	lanes	pushy

Part 1: Idioms

An **idiom** is a statement or phrase that doesn't mean exactly what the words say. People in different places have different ways of saying things. For example, to say that a person "has a green thumb" does not mean that his thumb is the color green. It means that this person is able to grow plants very easily. "Has a green thumb" is an idiom.

A. Each sentence below has an underlined idiom. Use the words around the idiom to help you figure out what the idiom means. Then read the list of definitions below. Write the letter of the definition that matches the idiom in the line behind the sentence.

A. be afraid to do something
B. start something that should be left alone
C. very busy; lots to do
D. not good at something or clumsy
E. do the impossible

F. be mistaken
G. to be very calm; under control
H. figure someone out
I. to be upset over something small
G. to fool someone

1. Kenny often tricked the other racers. He <u>pulled the wool over their eyes</u>. _____

2. You couldn't talk to him about losing. It'd be <u>opening up a can of worms</u>. _____

3. Kenny was always <u>busy as a bee</u> just before a race. _____

4. Some of the other racers felt like they <u>had two left feet</u> when they raced him. _____

5. If Kenny had a small wreck, he didn't <u>cry over spilled milk</u>. _____

6. Even when going 175 miles per hour, Kenny was <u>cool as a cucumber</u>. _____

7. When he looked like he would lose, he'd <u>pull a rabbit out of his hat</u> and win. _____

8. Someone would be <u>barking up the wrong tree</u> to pick a fight with Kenny. _____

9. Kenny could <u>read</u> the other racers <u>like a book</u>. He knew what they'd do. _____

10. Other drivers would <u>get cold feet</u> when they saw Kenny was in the race. _____

Unit 7, Lesson 1

Part 2: Specialized Vocabulary

People who work in a special field, such as sports or science, use special words. They use a **specialized vocabulary** to talk about their subjects. For example, a musician might use the word **chorus**. When you come across specialized vocabulary, look at the words and sentences around the special word to help you figure out its meaning.

A. The following sentences have specialized vocabulary about swimming. The specialized vocabulary is in **bold**. Underline the words in the sentence that tell you what each bold word means. Then write a definition on the line.

1. When swimmers gather to compete, the event is called a **swim meet.**

   meaning: _____

2. Swimmers usually wear **goggles** to protect their eyes from chemicals in the water.

   meaning: _____

3. The pool is divided into **lanes** which are rows for each swimmer to swim in so that they don't bump into each other.

   meaning: _____

4. Often racers have **heats.** The winners of these earlier races get to compete in the **finals** later on in which the best swimmers race.

   meaning: _____

   meaning: _____

5. A swimmer who jumps into the water before the official signal is given a **false start.** Swimmers get only one false start and then must leave the race.

   meaning: _____

6. A **relay** is a race in which four swimmers make up a team and switch with each other during the race.

   meaning: _____

7. If someone starts to drown in a pool, a **lifeguard,** who is trained to save lives in the water, will jump in and pull the person to safety.

   meaning: _____

Unit 7, Lesson 1

Part 3: Context Clues

When you come to a word that you don't know, read the words near the unknown word carefully. These words may give you **context clues** that help you figure out what the unknown word means. One type of context clue is a **definition** or **restatement clue.** This type of clue tells the exact meaning of an unknown word. For example, in the sentences below you see that the definition of *irritating* means to get mad.

My friend is irritating me. She is really making me mad.

A. Look for definition clues. Write the definition of each **boldfaced** word on the line.

1. Kenny was **dazed** when he hit the wall. He was shocked and confused because of the accident.

   Dazed means _____.

2. Even when Kenny was young he was **cocky.** He was too self-confident and bragged about how good he was.

   Cocky means _____.

3. To drive fast requires good **reflexes.** The body must react quickly without the person planning or thinking about it.

   Reflexes means _____.

4. There were many different **courses,** or race tracks, that Kenny had to learn.

   Courses means _____.

5. Kenny was **pushy** his whole life. He was bold and always tried to get what he wanted.

   Pushy means _____.

6. When racing a motorcycle, one should not be **awkward,** or clumsy.

   Awkward means _____.

7. If Kenny lost a race, he was **depressed.** This sadness would pass quickly though.

   Depressed means _____.

8. When he was eighteen, Kenny signed a professional **contract**—a legal agreement with someone else.

   Contract means _____.

Unit 7, Lesson 2

Power Words

Look at the words below. Circle any that you think you may know. Be ready to tell the class what the word means. Also tell the class how you think you know that word.

amnesia	ignite	leisure	sponsor
contents	interval	logo	track
crew	lack	oral	welded

Part 1: Idioms

An **idiom** is a statement or phrase that doesn't mean exactly what the words say. People in different places have different ways of saying things. For example, to say that a person "has a green thumb" does not mean that his thumb is the color green. It means that this person is able to grow plants very easily. "Has a green thumb" is an idiom.

A. Each sentence below has an underlined idiom. Use the words around the idiom to help you figure out what the idiom means. Then read the list of definitions below. Write the letter of the definition that matches the idiom in the line behind the sentence.

A. very hungry
B. to be a traitor or mean to someone
C. unable to go forward or continue
D. to be very mad
E. unable to see

F. someone who stays up very late
G. someone who gets up early
H. to do something unexpected
I. very tired
G. easily angered

1. When I broke my sister's doll, she was <u>mad as a wet hen</u>. _____

2. Mr. Davis is an <u>early bird</u>. He's always at school by 6:30 in the morning. _____

3. Ricardo was <u>hungry as a horse</u>. He ate seven pieces of pizza. _____

4. When Rosa broke up with Tom, she <u>pulled the rug right out from under him</u>. _____

5. Steve <u>stabbed me in the back</u> when he asked my girlfriend out on a date. _____

6. I <u>hit the wall</u> on the second page of the math test. I was unable to continue. _____

7. Louisa is a <u>night owl</u>. She rarely comes home before 2:00 in the morning. _____

8. Mary is <u>blind as a bat</u> without her glasses. She better not try to drive. _____

9. Sam is so <u>hot-headed</u>. He gets mad at the smallest things. _____

10. I was <u>bushed</u> after three hours of football practice. _____

Part 2: Specialized Vocabulary

People who work in a special field, such as sports or science, use special words. They use a **specialized vocabulary** to talk about their subjects. For example, a doctor might use the word **operation.** When you come across specialized vocabulary, look at the words and sentences around the special word to help you figure out its meaning.

A. The following sentences have specialized vocabulary about car racing. The specialized vocabulary is in **bold.** Underline the words in the sentence that tell you what each bold word means. Then write a definition on the line.

1. Racing cars often compete on a **track,** which is a closed–off roadway built for the purpose of racing.

   meaning: _____

2. One type of raceway is the **oval track,** which is shaped like an egg.

   meaning: _____

3. Every racing team has a **crew** made up of mechanics who keep the car running.

   meaning: _____

4. When the driver stops during the race, he makes a **pit stop** by pulling into an area just off the track where his crew waits to fix or refuel the car.

   meaning: _____

5. Before the big race, drivers have **time trials** to see how fast they can go and the order in which they will start the final race.

   meaning: _____

6. Most drivers have a **sponsor.** A sponsor is usually a large business or corporation that pays for the car and team.

   meaning: _____

7. The sponsors put **logos,** or labels, on the car to advertise their company to the public.

   meaning: _____

8. The audience usually watches from the **grandstands**—the seats around the track.

   meaning: _____

Unit 7, Lesson 2

Part 3: Context Clues

When you come to a word that you don't know, read the words near the unknown word carefully. These words may give you **context clues** that help you figure out what the unknown word means. One type of context clue is a **definition** or **restatement clue**. This type of clue tells the exact meaning of an unknown word. For example, in the sentences below you see that the definition of *lazy* means "not willing to work."

> Tim is so lazy. He never helps out or does any work of any kind.

A. Look for definition clues. Write the definition of each **boldfaced** word on the line.

1. After eating, there was an **interval,** or period of time, before David began swimming.

    Interval means _____.

2. When a car engine starts, the gas is **ignited** or set on fire.

    Ignited means _____.

3. Each driver was given an **oral** test in which they had to speak to a judge about what they knew.

    Oral means _____.

4. If a driver hits his head, he could experience **amnesia** and lose his memory.

    Amnesia means _____.

5. The **contents** of a pool are water and chlorine.

    Contents means _____.

6. Many parts of a car are **welded.** This is a strong way of joining metal together.

    Welded means _____.

7. Some racers **lack** the skills to make it into the final race and go home early.

    Lack means _____.

8. After a race, most drivers need some **leisure** or free time just to relax.

    Leisure means _____.

Unit 7, Lesson 3

Power Words Review

Look at the words below. Circle any that you think you may know. Be ready to tell the class what the word means. Try to use the word in a sentence to show its meaning.

amnesia	crew	interval	reflexes
awkward	dazed	lack	relay
cocky	depressed	lanes	sponsor
contents	finals	leisure	pushy
contract	goggles	logo	track
courses	ignite	oral	welded

Part 1: Idioms

An **idiom** is a statement or phrase that doesn't mean exactly what the words say. People in different places have different ways of saying things.

A. Match the idiom in **Column A** with its meaning in **Column B**. Write the letter of the correct meaning in the blank provided.

Column A

1. _____ early bird

2. _____ hit the wall

3. _____ read like a book

4. _____ get cold feet

5. _____ stabbed in the back

6. _____ hot-headed

7. _____ night owl

8. _____ open up a can of worms

9. _____ cool as a cucumber

10. _____ two left feet

11. _____ bushed

12. _____ cry over spilled milk

Column B

A. very tired

B. to be very calm; under control

C. be afraid to do something

D. to be upset over something small

E. very easily angered

F. clumsy or awkward

G. unable to go forward or continue

H. to figure someone out

I. to be a traitor or mean to someone

J. someone who gets up or arrives early

K. start something that should be left alone

L. someone who stays up very late

Unit 7, Lesson 3

Part 2: Specialized Vocabulary

People who work in a special field, such as sports or science, use special words. They use a **specialized vocabulary** to talk about their subjects. When you come across specialized vocabulary, look at the words and sentences around the special word to help you figure out its meaning.

A. Match the terms below with the picture. Write the correct term in the blank provided.

oval track   crew   pit stop

time trials   sponsor   logo

grandstands

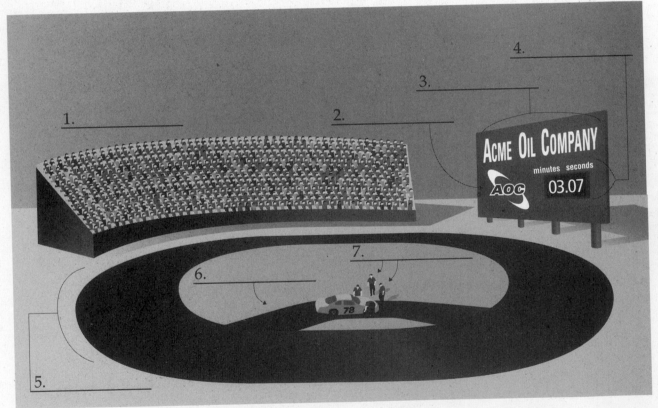

B. Fluency: Practice reading the following paragraph until you can read it smoothly. Then underline the seven specialized vocabulary words or phrases about swimming.

Jeff was very excited about the upcoming swim meet. As a former lifeguard, he was a very good athlete. He adjusted his goggles as he stood in front of his lane. The heats were over now. This race was the finals. He was in the 500 meter relay. Jeff leaned over the water, making sure he didn't false start. The gun sounded and he jumped in.

Unit 7, Lesson 3

Part 3: Context Clues

Remember that **context clues** help you figure out what an unknown word means. One type of context clue is a **definition clue**. This type of clue tells the exact meaning of an unknown word. A **restatement clue** gives a synonym, or word with nearly the same meaning as the unknown word.

A. In the blank provided, write the word defined by the restatement clue or phrase in **bold.** Use a dictionary if necessary. Use the words below for your answers.

tracks	interval	pushy	awkward
contents	ignited	leisure	depressed
amnesia	reflexes	welded	contract
lack	cocky	dazed	

1. The building **started on fire,** or _____, when the lightning hit it.

2. Kenny was very **stubborn and always tried to have things his way,** or _____.

3. The shop teacher **joined,** or _____ the pieces of **metal together.**

4. Race drivers have to get used to a number of different **courses,** or _____.

5. We enjoy having **free time,** or _____, when we travel.

6. When you first start to dance you feel very **clumsy,** or _____.

7. The **things inside,** or _____, of my lunch bag are scary.

8. The musician waited a **period of time,** or _____, before playing again.

9. When playing volleyball, your body must have quick _____, that is you must **be able to react quickly without thinking.**

10. When Rebecca hit her head, she got _____ and **lost her memory** for a day.

11. Kim was so **sad** and _____ when her boyfriend left for summer vacation.

12. If you **don't have,** or _____, certain skills you won't be able to ski.

13. I was **shocked and confused,** completely _____ the day the room filled with smoke.

14. The athlete signed **a legal agreement,** or _____, to play with the local team.

15. Sam is **over confident and bragging** about how good he is. He's _____.

Unit 7, Test

Part A: Idioms

Directions: Match the idiom in **Column A** with its meaning in **Column B**. Write the letter of the correct definition in the blank provided.

Column A

1. _____ hot-headed

2. _____ bushed

3. _____ two left feet

4. _____ cry over spilled milk

5. _____ cool as a cucumber

6. _____ hungry as a horse

7. _____ barking up the wrong tree

8. _____ read like a book

9. _____ stab someone in the back

10. _____ night owl

11. _____ pull the rug out from under

12. _____ open up a can of worms

13. _____ hit the wall

14. _____ busy as a bee

15. _____ pulled the wool over his eyes

Column B

A. to be a traitor or mean to someone

B. very busy

C. start something that should be left alone

D. someone who stays up very late

E. very hungry

F. unable to go forward or continue

G. very easily angered

H. to fool someone

I. to be very calm; under control

J. very tired

K. to be upset over something small

L. to figure someone out

M. to be mistaken

N. to do something unexpected or surprising

O. very clumsy

Name _____ Date _____

Part B: Specialized Vocabulary

Directions: The crossword puzzle below can be filled in with specialized vocabulary from swimming and car racing. Read the clues and fill in the puzzle.

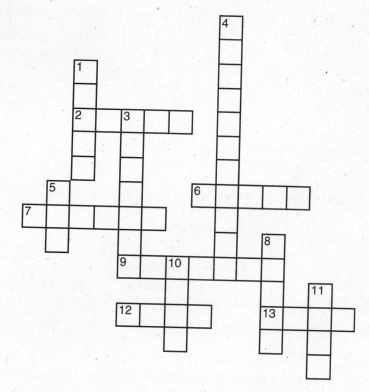

Across

2. labels for a company
6. the rows in a pool for swimmers
7. the last races with the best athletes
9. a large business that supports racing
12. early race to determine who continues on
13. the people who keep a racing car running

Down

1. a team of racers who take turns racing
3. water-proof glasses for swimmers
4. the seats for people watching an event
5. the place where racing cars stop for fuel
8. the roadway used for racing
10. an egg-shaped racing track
11. a swimming competition

Unit 7, Test

Part C: Context Clues

Directions: For each numbered blank, there is a list of words with the same number. Choose the word from each list that best completes the meaning of the paragraph.

1. My brother is very _____. He can react quickly without thinking, so he brags
   (1)
   about his _____.
   (2)

	1.		2.	
	○ awkward		○ contents	
	○ stupid		○ eflexes	
	○ cocky		○ attitude	
	○ smart		○ will power	

2. We were given an _____ test. We had to answer all the questions out loud and
   (3)
   only got to rest for one short _____ of ten minutes.
   (4)

	3.		4.	
	○ old		○ finals	
	○ oral		○ lesson	
	○ interval		○ interval	
	○ stupid		○ practice	

3. Justine is very _____. She messed up her presentation for the job, and the big
   (5)
   company will not make a _____ for her.
   (6)

	5.		6.	
	○ smart		○ contract	
	○ cocky		○ relay	
	○ wicked		○ school	
	○ depressed		○ vacation	

4. Mike was _____ after the car accident. Shocked and confused, he had _____
   (7)   (8)
   and could not remember anything for a while.

	7.		8.	
	○ pushy		○ track	
	○ riding		○ amnesia	
	○ dazed		○ school	
	○ fine		○ travels	

Unit 8, Lesson 1

Power Words

Look at the words below. Circle any that you think you may know. Be ready to tell the class what the word means. Also tell the class how you think you know that word.

comical	crane	intrigued	spring
conceal	fireplace	smuggle	thorough
courtyard	floorboards	spare	torture

Part 1: Multiple-Meaning Words

The word *multiple* means many. **Multiple-meaning words** are words that have more than one meaning. For example, the word *box* can mean to fight someone. It can also be a square container to put things in.

A. Read each sentence below. Think about how the **boldfaced** word in the sentence is used. Then read the different meanings of that word below. Write the letter of the definition in the blank that matches the meaning of the bold word in the sentence.

_____ 1. A **crane** was brought in to tear down the old building.
    a. a machine to move heavy objects up in the air
    b. a bird with a long neck and legs

_____ 2. Without the building, the **block** looked like it was missing a tooth.
    a. a solid piece of a hard substance
    b. a square section of a city bounded on each side by streets
    c. something that gets in the way; an obstacle

_____ 3. We wanted to **watch** the building fall from our apartment.
    a. the members of a ship's crew on duty for a period of time
    b. to look on or observe
    c. a small, portable timepiece often worn on the wrist

_____ 4. In place of the building, a group decided to build a **park** and garden.
    a. a piece of land set aside for recreation and plants with few buildings
    b. to put a vehicle, such as a car, in a location for a period of time

_____ 5. Everyone put as much time into fixing up the park as they could **spare.**
    a. a replacement, such as a tire for a car
    b. to give of one's time and resources

_____ 6. When **spring** came, there were flowers and vegetables in the new park.
    a. to jump up quickly
    b. a place where water flows out of the earth
    c. one of the four seasons that occurs after winter

Unit 8, Lesson 1

Part 2: Context Clues

Remember that you can often figure out the meaning of an unknown word from the words that appear nearby. The words or phrases that surround an unknown word are called **context clues.** For example, see how the words in the sentences below tell you that *menace* means dangerous.

The poisonous snake is a menace. It is dangerous and may hurt someone.

A. Use context clues to figure out the meaning of the **boldfaced** word. Darken in the circle with the correct definition.

1. The Frenchmen decided to try to **smuggle** the map away without the Nazis knowing.
   - ○ drive
   - ○ take secretly
   - ○ burn
   - ○ copy quietly

2. The map was too big to **conceal** under their jackets or in their pockets.
   - ○ sell
   - ○ sew
   - ○ convert
   - ○ hide

4. The guards gave the men a **thorough** search, looking through everything.
   - ○ wistful
   - ○ quick
   - ○ careful
   - ○ hasty

2. The Frenchmen were **intrigued** with the unusual idea of stealing the map.
   - ○ interested
   - ○ saddened
   - ○ bored
   - ○ calmed

5. Each man knew that if the soldiers caught him, he would undergo painful **torture.**
   - ○ sleep
   - ○ conversations
   - ○ suffering
   - ○ thoughts

6. Dressed as a silly rat catcher, the Frenchman looked quite **comical.**
   - ○ serious
   - ○ wealthy
   - ○ old
   - ○ funny

Unit 8, Lesson 1

Part 3: Compound Words

A **compound word** is a word made by putting two words together. Knowing the meaning of the smaller words helps you figure out the meaning of the whole word. For example, **ballpark** is made of the smaller words *ball* and *park*. You can figure out that a ballpark is a green area for playing ball.

A. Combine each word in **Row 1** with a word in **Row 2** to make a compound word. Then write each compound word beside its definition below.

Row 1:   bed   sun   cover   fire   floor

Row 2:   light   place   boards   room   alls

1. the light from the sun _____

2. work clothes that cover other clothing _____

3. a room in which one sleeps _____

4. pieces of wood that make up a floor _____

5. a place in a house where fires are kept _____

B. Use a compound word from Exercise A to complete the following sentences. Then, see if you can find the other compound word in each sentence and circle it.

1. The men could see the castle courtyard from their _____.

2. As he warmed by the _____ he was glad he wasn't outdoors.

3. Seeing the bright _____, she knew she didn't need a raincoat.

4. The carpenter used driftwood in the _____ of the beach house.

5. As a joke, my brother wore his work _____ to my birthday party.

6. We were wide-awake when the bright _____ streamed in.

7. The painter became short-tempered when he spilled paint on his _____.

8. Robert sat by the _____ to keep warm in the cold house.

9. My grandmother hides her money under the wooden _____.

10. I sleep beside the windowpane in my _____.

Unit 8, Lesson 2

Power Words

Look at the words below. Circle any that you think you may know. Be ready to tell the class what the word means. Also tell the class how you think you know that word.

client	fingerprint	overly	thick
double-cross	modified	regard	wake
evil-looking	nourishment	stopwatch	well-heeled

Part 1: Multiple-Meaning Words

The word *multiple* means many. **Multiple-meaning words** are words that have more than one meaning. For example, the word *meal* can mean food served and eaten at a sitting. It can also be a ground-up grain, such as corn meal.

A. Read each sentence below. Think about how the **boldfaced** word in the sentence is used. Then read the different meanings of that word below. Write the letter of the definition in the blank that matches the meaning of the bold word in the sentence.

_____ 1. The Frenchman did not know where to put the **thick** map.
   a. dull or stupid
   b. heavy in form or size

_____ 2. The map was too large to **hide** in his pocket.
   a. the skin of an animal
   b. to put out of sight; to conceal

_____ 3. Even if he took out the other **stuff** from his pocket, the map still wouldn't fit.
   a. a collection of objects, many of which are worthless
   b. to pack tightly or to fill

_____ 4. It was at the city **dump** that he got an idea.
   a. to empty material out of a container
   b. a place where garbage is put
   c. to criticize someone severely

_____ 5. He changed his identification **tag** to look like that of a rat catcher.
   a. a strip of leather, paper, metal, or plastic attached to something
   b. a children's game
   c. to touch a runner with the ball in baseball so that the runner is out

_____ 6. Then he went to **wake** up the rats.
   a. the track of waves in the water left behind a boat
   b. a watch over a dead person at a funeral
   c. to stop sleeping

Unit 8, Lesson 2

Part 2: Context Clues

Remember that you can often figure out the meaning of an unknown word from the words that appear nearby. The words or phrases that surround an unknown word are called **context clues.** For example, see how the words in the sentences below tell you that *idiotic* means stupid.

Jeff can be very idiotic. He does the stupidest things most of the time.

A. Use context clues to figure out the meaning of the **boldfaced** word. Darken in the circle with the correct definition.

1. Sara is **overly** polite. She says "Thank you" and "You're Welcome" too many times.
   - ○ somewhat
   - ○ occasionally
   - ○ too
   - ○ mostly

2. The road had been **modified** and now turned right instead of left as it once did.
   - ○ repaved
   - ○ saved
   - ○ tunneled
   - ○ changed

3. The shopkeeper was glad to get a new **client** who would buy his goods.
   - ○ customer
   - ○ salesman
   - ○ office
   - ○ worker

4. We hadn't eaten all day and looked forward to some good **nourishment.**
   - ○ clothing
   - ○ food
   - ○ fun
   - ○ weather

5. The players loved their coach and viewed him with great **regard.**
   - ○ patience
   - ○ fun
   - ○ respect
   - ○ thoughts

6. You may want me to leave; **nevertheless,** I am staying.
   - ○ seriously
   - ○ even so
   - ○ because
   - ○ afterwards

Unit 8, Lesson 2

Part 3: Compound Words

Remember that a **compound word** is a word made by putting two words together. Knowing the meaning of the smaller words helps you figure out the meaning of the whole word. Sometimes a compound word has a hyphen (-). For example, the compound word *half-mile* is hyphenated.

A. Combine each word in **Row 1** with a word in **Row 2** to make a compound word. Then write each compound word beside its definition below.

Row 1: well-   evil-   finger   double-   stop

Row 2: looking   cross   watch   print   heeled

1. someone who appears to be mean   _____

2. the mark left on a surface from a finger   _____

3. having plenty of money   _____

4. to fool or trick in a mean way   _____

5. a timepiece that can be stopped by hand   _____

B. Fluency: Practice reading the paragraph below until you can read it smoothly. Then find the 17 compound words in the paragraph. Circle each word. Remember that some compound words are hyphenated.

Maria was a seventh-grader when she joined the track team. Her teammates didn't like her at first. Maria had come from a farm. The other runners asked her if she ran around the cornfield. Maria said she didn't have time because she was always working in the barnyard. She became a good runner from running the half-mile to the mailbox every day. Her team laughed at her. They were well-heeled and ran on tracks in buildings.

Then the day came for the first race. The starter fired the gunshot to begin the race. At the beginning of the race Maria was in twenty-third place. Maria was afraid another runner might double-cross her. She was used to running outside, however. When the timekeeper stopped the stopwatch at the halfway point, Maria was catching up. By the final lap, Maria was in first place. The other runners congratulated her. She certainly won her self-respect back. The team realized she was not a small-town person. They named her the "wildcat" because she ran so fast.

Unit 8, Lesson 3

Power Words Review

Look at the words below. Circle any that you think you may know. Be ready to tell the class what the word means. Also tell the class how you think you know that word.

client	evil-looking	nourishment	stopwatch
comical	fingerprint	overly	thick
conceal	fireplace	regard	thorough
courtyard	floorboards	smuggle	torture
crane	intrigued	spare	wake
double-cross	modified	spring	well-heeled

Part 1: Multiple-Meaning Words

Multiple-meaning words are words that have more than one meaning.

A. Read each sentence below. Find the word that fits in both sentences.

1. Dad pulled the _____ out of the trunk to fix the flat tire on the car.

   Serena said she could _____ some time to study her history.
   - take
   - tire
   - spare
   - spring

2. Juan did not know where to _____ when the monster chased him.

   The hunter killed the tiger and kept its _____.
   - stuff
   - run
   - go
   - hide

3. My sister always falls when she water-skis over the _____ behind the boat.

   I did not hear my alarm clock and didn't _____ in time for class.
   - wake
   - block
   - water
   - spring

4. The _____ on the suitcase said it was my grandfather's.

   The shortstop was able to _____ the runner before he got back to the base.
   - hide
   - spring
   - tag
   - label

Unit 8, Lesson 3

Part 2: Context Clues

Remember that you can often figure out the meaning of an unknown word from the words that appear nearby. The words or phrases that surround an unknown word are called **context clues**.

A. Use context clues to figure out the meaning of the **boldfaced** word. Darken in the circle with the correct definition.

1. Without proper **nourishment,** one will grow weak and die.
   - ○ regard
   - ○ food
   - ○ rest
   - ○ clothing

2. Sharon was **intrigued** to learn about her family history.
   - ○ interested
   - ○ happy
   - ○ comical
   - ○ saddened

3. My cousin is **overly** mean to me. He makes fun of me and hits me.
   - ○ somewhat
   - ○ quickly
   - ○ thoroughly
   - ○ too

4. I hold my teacher in great **regard** because she works so hard and is so smart.
   - ○ conceal
   - ○ energy
   - ○ respect
   - ○ calm

5. The policeman gave a **thorough** search to look for stolen goods.
   - ○ careful
   - ○ slick
   - ○ modified
   - ○ hasty

6. Jon was embarrassed and tried to **conceal** his pleasure when he won the award.
   - ○ regard
   - ○ show
   - ○ hide
   - ○ ignore

Unit 8, Lesson 3

Part 3: Compound Words

A **compound word** is a word made by putting two words together. Knowing the meaning of the smaller words helps you figure out the meaning of the whole word

A. Use the clues below to fill in the Crossword Puzzle. All the answers are compound words you have studied in this unit.

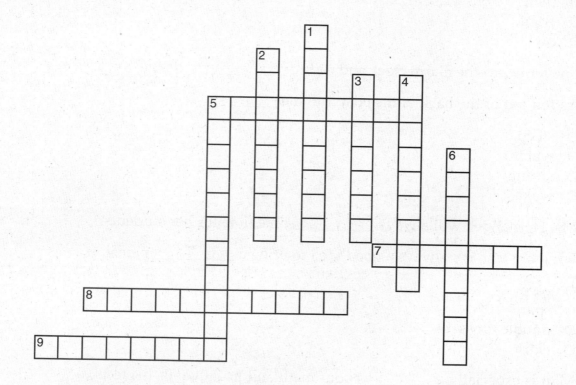

Across

5. a place where fires are kept
7. a room in which one sleeps
8. mark left by a finger
9. outside

Down

1. a time piece that can be stopped
2. the yard on a farm near the barn
3. a container where letters are put
4. members of the same team
5. pieces of wood that make up a floor
6. work clothes that cover other clothes

Unit 8, Test

Part A: Multiple-Meaning Words

Directions: Read each sentence below. Find the word that fits in both sentences.

1. The huge _____ lifted the boards over the building.

   We saw a long-billed _____ flying over the river.

   - ○ truck
   - ○ plane
   - ○ crane
   - ○ owl

2. I never heard the alarm clock and didn't _____ .

   Ira fell out of the back of the boat into the _____ .

   - ○ sleep
   - ○ water
   - ○ spring
   - ○ wake

3. Ms. Hernandez will always _____ some time for her students.

   For a big test, it's always a good idea to bring a _____ pencil.

   - ○ give
   - ○ spare
   - ○ double-cross
   - ○ extra

4. Matt is especially _____ about math and usually fails his tests.

   On payday, my wallet is _____ with money.

   - ○ thick
   - ○ well-heeled
   - ○ spare
   - ○ good

5. We found a beautiful _____ in the woods by our campground.

   The firemen were ready to _____ into action when the alarm went off.

   - ○ crane
   - ○ wake
   - ○ spring
   - ○ deer

Unit 8, Test

Part B: Context Clues

Directions: For each numbered blank, there is a list of words with the same number. Choose the word from each list that best completes the meaning of the paragraph.

1. The _____ was angry at the shopkeeper. He had tried to _____ the high
   (1)   (2)
   price of the clothes in his store from his customers.

    1.   ○ chef   **2.**   ○ spring
         ○ client   ○ torture
         ○ crane   ○ conceal
         ○ spare   ○ regard

2. My sister didn't like the _____ she was getting. The cook had _____ the
   (3)   (4)
   meals in the restaurant from mild to very hot foods.

    3.   ○ money   **4.**   ○ smuggled
         ○ client   ○ modified
         ○ torture   ○ sold
         ○ nourishment   ○ wished

3. The unusual and interesting setting _____ Jan. This was the first time she had
   (5)
   been to a comedy club, and she found the comedians very _____.
                                                             (6)

    5.   ○ bored   **6.**   ○ spare
         ○ tortured   ○ comical
         ○ evil-looking   ○ boring
         ○ intrigued   ○ sad

4. The robbers had tried to _____ stuff. After a _____ search, however, the
   (7)   (8)
   police were able to find everything they had hidden in the shipping boxes.

    7.   ○ buy   **8.**   ○ thick
         ○ spare   ○ thorough
         ○ regard   ○ bad
         ○ smuggle   ○ comical

Unit 8, Test

Part C: Compound Words

Directions: Match the compound word in **Column A** with its meaning in **Column B**. Write the letter of the correct definition in the blank provided.

Column A

1. _____ double-cross

2. _____ teammate

3. _____ floorboards

4. _____ barnyard

5. _____ bedroom

6. _____ evil-looking

7. _____ stopwatch

8. _____ timekeeper

9. _____ well-heeled

10. _____ fireplace

11. _____ sunlight

12. _____ fingerprint

13. _____ coveralls

14. _____ mailbox

15. _____ self-respect

Column B

A. a person on the same team as another

B. work clothes worn over other clothes

C. the light from the sun

D. very wealthy

E. a place in a home where fires are built

F. the room in which one sleeps

G. a box for receiving letters or mail

H. wooden boards that are used in floors

I. to trick someone in a mean way

J. appearing mean or nasty

K. feeling good about one's self

L. the mark left by a finger

M. someone who keeps track of time

N. the field or yard around a barn

O. a timepiece that can be stopped

Name _____   Date _____

Power Words

Look at the words below. Circle any that you think you may know. Be ready to tell the class what the word means. Also tell the class how you think you know that word.

admit	geology	ointment	temperamental
collapse	irregular	phonograph	thermos
commit	mechanic	telescope	transport

Part 1: Prefixes

A **prefix** is a word part added to the beginning of a word. A prefix can also be added to a **root** to form a new word. Remember that a root is a word that cannot stand alone. For example, in the word **transfer,** the prefix *trans* means "across" and *fer* is a Latin root that means "to carry." When you put the prefix and root together you get "to carry across." Today, we use the word transfer to mean "to move or carry from one place to another." Study the meaning of the following prefixes until you can remember what each means.

> *sub-* means "below" / *super-* means "above" or "beyond" / *ir-* means "not"
> *trans-* means "across" / *col-, com-, con-,* and *cor-* mean "with" or "together"

A. For each word below, draw a line between the prefix and the root or base word. Then write what the word means on the line. Use a dictionary if necessary.

1. superhuman - _____

2. conform - _____

3. transplant - _____

4. irregular - _____

5. submarine - _____

6. collapse - _____

7. supercharge - _____

8. commit - _____

9. irresponsible - _____

10. transport - _____

11. correspond - _____

12. subway - _____

Unit 9, Lesson 1

Part 2: Greek and Latin Roots

Many English words are made up of word parts from other languages, especially Greek and Latin. These word parts are called **roots**. A root cannot stand alone, but knowing its meaning helps you figure out the meaning of the whole word. A group of words with the same root is called a **word family.** Study the chart of **Greek** roots below.

Root	Meaning	Example
phon	sound	telephone
geo	earth	geography
tele	far, distant	telescope
therm	heat	thermos
mech	machine	mechanic

A. Match the word in **Column A** with its correct meaning in **Column B.** Write the letter of the correct meaning in the space provided. Use a dictionary if necessary.

Column A

1. _____ phonograph

2. _____ television

3. _____ thermos

4. _____ geology

5. _____ mechanic

6. _____ thermal

7. _____ telephone

8. _____ geography

9. _____ mechanize

10. _____ telescope

Column B

A. a person who works on machines

B. the study of the earth's rocks

C. a device to see far away objects

D. to add machinery to something

E. a machine that plays records

F. a device that transmits sound signals

G. a device that keeps liquids warm or cool

H. a machine that receives visual images

J. the study of the earth and the life on it

K. related to or caused by heat

Unit 9, Lesson 1

Part 3: Shades of Meaning

Words may have small differences in meaning. A reader must know the exact meaning of a word to understand what the writer is saying. For example, a dinner that is *grand* is different from a dinner that is *nice*. Grand is much better than nice.

A. Read the sentence with the missing word. Then read the question about the missing word. Choose the word that best answers the question.

1. The skateboarder put the _____ on her scratch to help it heal.

   Which of these words would indicate that the skateboarder put a healing cream on her scratch?

   A. band aid
   B. powder
   C. ointment
   D. vitamin

2. Our class went downtown to hear a famous _____.

   Which of these words would indicate that the class heard a musical composition?

   A. band
   B. symphony
   C. DJ
   D. composer

3. After waiting in line for an hour, Jim was finally _____ to the baseball game.

   Which of these words would indicate that Jim was finally let in to the baseball game?

   A. admitted
   B. helped
   C. driven
   D. asked

4. Kim had a very _____ coach who yelled a lot.

   Which of these words would indicate that Kim's coach is easily angered?

   A. bold
   B. unfair
   C. temperamental
   D. nervous

Unit 9, Lesson 2

Power Words

Look at the words below. Circle any that you think you may know. Be ready to tell the class what the word means. Also tell the class how you think you know that word.

abundance	dependence	inspect	recede
brotherhood	exiled	interrupt	tarnish
confidence	impulsively	racism	transform

Part 1: Suffixes

A **suffix** is a word part added to the end of a word. A suffix can help you determine a word's part of speech. You remember that a noun is the name of a person, place, or thing. When you add the suffix **ness** to the adjective *kind,* it becomes the noun *kind-ness.* Study the following suffixes. Each suffix can turn a word or word part into a noun.

-ance as in appear<u>ance</u> / *-ence* as in differ<u>ence</u> /
-ism as in rac<u>ism</u> / *-hood* as in neighbor<u>hood</u> / *-ness* as in good<u>ness</u>

A. For each word below, draw a line between the suffix and the root or base word. Then write what the word means on the line. Use a dictionary if necessary.

1. confidence - _____

2. sameness - _____

3. racism - _____

4. brotherhood - _____

5. dependence - _____

6. realism - _____

7. defiance - _____

8. student - _____

9. motherhood - _____

10. obedience - _____

11. abundance - _____

12. residence - _____

Unit 9, Lesson 2

Part 2: Greek and Latin Roots

Many English words are made up of word parts from other languages, especially Greek and Latin. These word parts are called **roots**. A root cannot stand alone, but knowing its meaning helps you figure out the meaning of the whole word. A group of words with the same root is called a **word family**. Study the chart of **Latin** roots below.

Root	Meaning	Example
form	form or shape	uni<u>form</u>
rupt	break	inter<u>rupt</u>
cede, ceed, cess	go, yield, give away	re<u>cess</u>
spec, spect, spic	look, see	<u>spec</u>tacles
trac, tract	pull, move	<u>tract</u>or

A. Match the word in **Column A** with its correct meaning in **Column B**. Write the letter of the correct meaning in the space provided. Use a dictionary if necessary.

Column A

1. _____ recess

2. _____ interrupt

3. _____ inspect

4. _____ tractor

5. _____ disrupt

6. _____ recede

7. _____ succeed

8. _____ transform

9. _____ spectacles

10. _____ erupt

Column B

A. to look at closely; to examine

B. glasses to improve one's sight

C. to break into another's conversation

D. to do well or go ahead, to accomplish

E. to explode or burst forth

F. to change something

G. to stop the progress of, to disturb

H. a vehicle used in farming

J. to go back from a set point

K. a temporary break or stop

Unit 9, Lesson 2

Part 3: Shades of Meaning

Words may have small differences in meaning. A reader must know the exact meaning of a word to understand what the writer is saying. For example, a dinner that is *grand* is different from a dinner that is *nice*. Grand is much better than nice.

A. Read the sentence with the missing word. Then read the question about the missing word. Choose the word that best answers the question.

1. The baseball player swung _____ at every ball thrown to him and struck out.

   Which of these words would indicate that the baseball player swung without thinking?

   A. angrily
   B. impulsively
   C. quickly
   D. occasionally

2. The skateboard wheels were _____ from having sat in the rain for two weeks.

   Which of these words would indicate that the wheels were discolored?

   A. stuck
   B. cracked
   C. tarnished
   D. worn

3. The karate champ was _____ from the country when he hurt someone badly.

   Which of these words would indicate that karate champ was forcefully sent out of the country?

   A. tried
   B. helped
   C. exiled
   D. asked

4. Our teacher _____ our tests in ABC order in the cabinet.

   Which of these words would indicate that the teacher arranged the tests for storage?

   A. filed
   B. graded
   C. wrote
   D. passed out

Unit 9, Lesson 3

Power Words Review

Look at the words below. Circle any that you think you may know. Be ready to tell the class what the word means. Also tell the class how you think you know that word.

abundance	dependence	interrupt	tarnish
admit	exiled	mechanic	telescope
brotherhood	geology	ointment	temperamental
collapse	impulsively	phonograph	thermos
commit	irregular	racism	transport
confidence	inspect	recede	

Part 1: Prefixes and Suffixes

Remember that prefixes and suffixes are called **affixes**. Adding an affix to a word or root changes the word's meaning or part of speech. Study the meaning of the following prefixes and suffixes until you can remember what each means.

sub- means "below" / *super-* means "above" or "beyond" / *ir-* means "not"
trans- means "across" / *col, com, con,* and *cor* mean "with" or "together"
-ance as in appear<u>ance</u> / *-ence* as in differ<u>ence</u> /
-ism as in rac<u>ism</u> / *-hood* as in neighbor<u>hood</u> / *-ness* as in good<u>ness</u>

A. Match the word in **Column A** with its meaning in **Column B**.

Column A

1. _____ superhuman
2. _____ brotherhood
3. _____ transplant
4. _____ dependence
5. _____ submarine
6. _____ confidence
7. _____ irregular
8. _____ racism
9. _____ abundance
10. _____ collapse
11. _____ commit
12. _____ kindness

Column B

A. the state of needing or depending on someone
B. a dislike of people of other races or ethnic groups
C. a good feeling about oneself and one's abilities
D. to make up one's mind to do something
E. nor regular or normal
F. to fall down or cave in
G. to move from one place to another
H. an act of or feeling from doing good things
I. above or beyond normal or human
J. a vessel designed to move underwater
K. a great or large amount of something
L. a feeling of togetherness

Unit 9, Lesson 3

Part 2: Greek and Latin Roots

Many English words are made up of word parts from other languages, especially Greek and Latin. These word parts are called **roots.** Study the chart of roots below.

Root	Meaning	Example
phon	sound	tele<u>phon</u>e
geo	earth	<u>geo</u>graphy
tele	far, distant	<u>tele</u>scope
therm	heat	<u>therm</u>os
mech	machine	<u>mech</u>anic
form	form or shape	uni<u>form</u>
rupt	break	inter<u>rupt</u>
cede, ceed, cess	go, yield, give away	re<u>cess</u>
spec, spect, spic	look, see	<u>spec</u>tacles
trac, tract	pull, move	<u>trac</u>tor

A. Fluency: Practice reading the selection below until you can read it smoothly. Find the 13 words that have roots from the chart above. Draw a line between the root and the rest of the word.

Chris, a mechanic, was called in to inspect the telescope at the university. Chris said his work would disrupt the teacher's classes. So, the teacher told the students to take a recess. After everyone left, Chris put on his spectacles and looked at the machine.

Chris worked hard all morning. The machine was so big he used a tractor to pull it out of its frame. Then he began to transform the machine. He realized that the thermal heat from the sun made the machine too hot. But, each day when the sun would recede, the machine would cool off. He didn't know what to do.

He sat down in the shade and opened his thermos to drink some coffee. That's when he got an idea. He telephoned his brother who brought over a big sun screen. Once he set it up, he knew his idea would succeed. The machine worked perfectly.

Unit 9, Lesson 3

Part 3: Shades of Meaning

Words may have small differences in meaning. A reader must know the exact meaning of a word to understand what the writer is saying. For example, a dinner that is grand is different from a dinner that is nice. Grand is much better than nice.

A. Read the sentence with the missing word. Then read the question about the missing word. Choose the word that best answers the question.

1. Juan was very angry and answered his mom _____.

   Which of these words would indicate that Juan answered his mom without thinking?

   A. angrily
   B. quietly
   C. impulsively
   D. weirdly

2. The old car was _____ from sitting outside for so long.

   Which of these words would indicate that the old car was discolored?

   A. tarnished
   B. dead
   C. stuck
   D. cracked

3. Sally was _____ to the hospital after her car accident.

   Which of these words would indicate that Sally was let in the hospital?

   A. driven
   B. helped
   C. admitted
   D. asked

4. Tillie's boss was _____ and yelled at his employees.

   Which of these words would indicate that Tillie's boss was easily angered?

   A. crazy
   B. unfair
   C. passionate
   D. temperamental

Unit 9, Test

Part A: Prefixes and Suffixes

Directions: Fill in the letter of the word that most nearly matches the meaning of the underlined word.

1. a feeling of <u>brotherhood</u>
    Ⓐ anger
    Ⓑ togetherness
    Ⓒ truth
    Ⓓ rivalry
    Ⓔ sincerity

2. great <u>abundance</u>
    Ⓕ desire
    Ⓖ job
    Ⓗ imagination
    Ⓘ wealth
    Ⓙ ability

3. a <u>superhuman</u> job
    Ⓚ good
    Ⓛ normal
    Ⓜ regular
    Ⓝ human
    Ⓞ incredible

4. we <u>correspond</u>
    Ⓟ play
    Ⓠ work
    Ⓡ write
    Ⓢ talk
    Ⓣ sleep

5. with <u>kindness</u>
    Ⓐ niceness
    Ⓑ playfulness
    Ⓒ medicine
    Ⓓ luck
    Ⓔ truthfulness

6. an <u>irregular</u> performance
    Ⓕ silly
    Ⓖ wonderful
    Ⓗ quick
    Ⓘ uneven
    Ⓙ normal

7. to <u>collapse</u>
    Ⓚ fight
    Ⓛ crumble
    Ⓜ fix
    Ⓝ struggle
    Ⓞ sleep

8. with <u>confidence</u>
    Ⓟ faith
    Ⓠ anger
    Ⓡ joy
    Ⓢ wishes
    Ⓣ hate

9. a <u>dependence</u>
    Ⓐ wish
    Ⓑ place
    Ⓒ buying
    Ⓓ home
    Ⓔ needing

10. due to <u>racism</u>
    Ⓕ reasons
    Ⓖ prejudice
    Ⓗ support
    Ⓘ government
    Ⓙ opinions

Unit 9, Test

Part B: Greek and Latin Roots

Directions: Match the meaning of the word in **Column B** with the word in **Column A**.

Column A

1. _____ mechanic
2. _____ inspect
3. _____ telescope
4. _____ interrupt
5. _____ recess
6. _____ spectacles
7. _____ tractor
8. _____ transport
9. _____ recede
10. _____ thermos
11. _____ geology
12. _____ phonograph

Column B.

A. the study of the earth's structure and rocks

B. to go back from a certain point

C. glasses to improve one's vision

D. a person who works on machines

E. to break into another's conversation

F. to carry or take from one place to another

G. to look at closely; to examine

H. a device for looking at things far away

I. a device for keeping liquids cool or warm

J. a machine for playing records

K. a vehicle used in farming

L. a temporary break or stop

Directions: Each Latin and Greek root below has two definitions. Only one is correct. Write the letter of the correct one on the blank provided.

1. _____ phon — A. machine — B. sound
2. _____ cede, ceed, cees — A. go, yield — B. see
3. _____ tele — A. far, distant — B. break
4. _____ trac, tract — A. pull, move — B. earth
5. _____ therm — A. machine — B. heat
6. _____ rupt — A. sound — B. break
7. _____ geo — A. look, see — B. earth
8. _____ spec, spect, spic — A. look, see — B. heat

Unit 9, Test

Part C: Shades of Meaning

Directions: Read the sentence with the missing word. Then read the question about the missing word. Choose the word that best answers the question.

1. The prince was _____ when he tried to kill the king.

   Which of these words would indicate that the prince was sent away?

   A. executed
   B. sad
   C. exiled
   D. injured

2. Vince will be _____ to class as soon as he shows up.

   Which of these words would indicate that Vince will be let in?

   A. exiled
   B. committed
   C. admitted
   D. tarnished

3. The chef is very _____ and yells at the other cooks.

   Which of these words would indicate that the chef gets angry easily.

   A. committed
   B. tarnished
   C. old
   D. temperamental

4. Mia's ring was _____ from having swum in the pool all summer.

   Which of these words would indicate that Mia's ring was discolored?

   A. tarnished
   B. exiled
   C. bent
   D. collapsed

5. When Ted saw the rat he acted _____ and jumped on the chair.

   Which of these words would indicate that Ted acted without thinking?

   A. dependence
   B. impulsively
   C. wisely
   D. confidently

Unit 10, Lesson 1

Power Words

Look at the words below. Circle any that you think you may know. Be ready to tell the class what the word means. Also tell the class how you think you know that word.

arms	count	falsehood	implore
brush	courage	famine	pole
check	determined	hide	runaway

Part 1: Multiple-Meaning Words

The word *multiple* means many. **Multiple-meaning words** are words that have more than one meaning. For example, the word *box* can mean to fight someone. It can also be a square container to put things in.

A. Read each sentence below. Think about how the **bold word** in the sentence is used. Then read the different meanings of that word below. Write the letter of the definition in the blank that matches the meaning of the bold word in the sentence.

_____ 1. Della decided to **count** her money so she could buy Jim a present.
    a. to have importance or to matter
    b. to add up one by one
    c. a nobleman in some foreign countries

_____ 2. Della decided to buy Jim a chain for his gold **watch**.
    a. to look or observe
    b. the job of standing guard
    c. a small, portable time piece often worn on the wrist or kept in a pocket

_____ 3. She put on her old brown **coat** and headed down the street.
    a. to cover with a layer of paint
    b. an outer piece of clothing with long sleeves

_____ 4. She went to the mirror to **check** her hair.
    a. a quick stop or halt
    b. a bill at a restaurant
    c. to inspect in order to determine accuracy or quantity
    d. to try to stop another player in ice hockey

_____ 5. Della found a **store** that would give her money for her long, beautiful hair.
    a. to fill or supply for future use
    b. a place where goods are sold

_____ 6. When Jim saw his new present, he took her in his **arms**.
    a. the upper limbs of the body
    b. weapons, especially firearms

Unit 10, Lesson 1

Part 2: Context Clues

Remember that you can often figure out the meaning of an unknown word from the words that appear nearby. The words or phrases that surround an unknown word are called **context clues**. For example, see how the words in the sentences below tell you that *frightening* means scary.

The poisonous snake is frightening. It scares everyone.

A. Use context clues to figure out the meaning of the **bold** word. Darken in the circle with the correct definition.

1. Many people tried to help **runaway** slaves as they ran to become free of their masters.
   - ○ old
   - ○ illegal
   - ○ escaped
   - ○ quiet

2. It took a lot of **courage** to hide a slave and face the mean slave hunters.
   - ○ intelligence
   - ○ bravery
   - ○ stupidity
   - ○ sense

3. Some people's religion teaches them to always tell the truth and not speak **falsehoods**.
   - ○ legends
   - ○ languages
   - ○ lies
   - ○ loudly

4. The people hiding the slaves would not be stopped; they were very **determined**.
   - ○ interested
   - ○ firm
   - ○ bored
   - ○ calm

5. Sometimes there is nothing to eat and people suffer a great **famine**.
   - ○ spread of fire
   - ○ spread of disease
   - ○ shortage of food
   - ○ loss of water

6. The slaves **implored** others to hide them so that they wouldn't be caught and beaten.
   - ○ begged
   - ○ wished
   - ○ asked
   - ○ told

Name _____   Date _____

Part 3: Using a Dictionary

A dictionary contains an alphabetical listing of words. Much information is provided about each word, or entry. Dictionaries tell you how to pronounce a word, its part of speech, and its meaning. Dictionaries may also tell you the history of the word. It may also give synonyms or words that mean almost the same thing. When you look up a word, use the context of what you are reading to help you choose the definition that makes the most sense.

A. In each of the sentences, one word is underlined. Find the word in the boxed dictionary entries below. Decide which meaning best matches the context, or ideas, in the sentence. Then write the part of speech and the definition on the lines provided.

Part of Speech   **Definition**

1. Allen had quite a <u>story</u> to tell when he got home.

   _____   _____

2. He had been out with his fishing <u>pole</u> trying to catch some dinner.

   _____   _____

3. Suddenly he heard a sound in the <u>brush</u> by the river.

   _____   _____

4. There he saw a runaway slave trying to <u>hide</u>.

   _____   _____

5. His clothes were so old they looked like the <u>hide</u> of a deer.

   _____   _____

---

brush 1 (brŭsh) *n.* **1.** A device with bristles attached to a handle and used for painting.— *v.* **2.** To clean, polish, or scrub with a brush.
brush 2 (brŭsh) *n.* **1.** A thick growth of bushes and trees.

hide 1 (hīd) *v.* **1.** To put or keep out of sight. **2.** To seek safety or refuge.
hide 2 (hīd) *n.* **1.** The skin of an animal.

pole 1 (pōl) *n.* **1.** Either of the regions at the top or bottom of the earth
pole 2 (pōl) *n.* **1.** A long, slender rounded piece of wood or other material.— *v.*
1. To push or propel oneself using a pole. **2.** *Sports.* To use ski poles to maintain or gain speed.

sto•ry 1 (stôr′ ē) *n.* **1.** An accout of an event or series of events. **2.** A newspaper article. **3.** A lie.
sto•ry 2 (stôr′ ē) *n.* **1.** A set of rooms on the same level of a building.

Unit 10, Lesson 2

Power Words

Look at the words below. Circle any that you think you may know. Be ready to tell the class what the word means. Also tell the class how you think you know that word.

deed	handle	needle	steep
fair	intend	raging	sterilize
grain	modest	splint	stretcher

Part 1: Multiple-Meaning Words

The word *multiple* means many. **Multiple-meaning words** are words that have more than one meaning. For example, the word *plant* can mean something that grows. It can also be a place where things are made or manufactured.

A. Read each sentence below. Think about how the bold word in the sentence is used. Then read the different meanings of that word below. Write the letter of the definition in the blank that matches the meaning of the bold word in the sentence.

_____ 1. The young prince thought he was very wise and **fair** in his decisions.
    a. having a pleasing appearance
    b. a gathering or exhibition at which people gather
    c. equal and just to all people

_____ 2. For many years the rice grew very **well** in his country.
    a. a deep hole sunk into the earth
    b. in a good or proper way

_____ 3. The prince decided to do a good **deed** for a girl in the village.
    a. an act or action
    b. a sealed document related to property

_____ 4. She said that all she wanted was one **grain** of rice.
    a. the pattern on the surface of a piece of wood
    b. a small, dry, one-seeded fruit of a cereal grass
    c. a very small amount

_____ 5. He told her she could have all the rice that fell into her **skirt.**
    a. one of the leather flaps hanging from a saddle
    b. to pass close by and narrowly miss
    c. a piece of clothing hanging from the waist and worn by women and girls

_____ 6. Eventually, she would leave the prince with only enough rice to fill a **bowl.**
    a. a wide vessel or rounded dish used to hold liquids
    b. to roll or throw a ball in sports

Part 2: Context Clues

Remember that you can often figure out the meaning of an unknown word from the words that appear nearby. The words or phrases that surround an unknown word are called **context clues**. For example, see how the words in the sentences below tell you that *postponed* means to delay until another date.

The game was postponed due to the rain. It was rescheduled for next Friday.

A. Use context clues to figure out the meaning of the **bold** word. Darken in the circle with the correct definition.

1. In old days, nurses only took a **modest** pay instead of a lot of money.
   - ○ small
   - ○ illegal
   - ○ large
   - ○ good

2. The nurse taped sticks to the sides of the leg to form a **splint** that would support it.
   - ○ shaft
   - ○ brace
   - ○ branch
   - ○ cane

3. The man had broken his leg in the **raging** river that was out of control.
   - ○ calm
   - ○ small
   - ○ large
   - ○ wild

4. Someday the nurse **intended** to build a hospital back in the woods for the people.
   - ○ hoped
   - ○ planned
   - ○ decided
   - ○ worked

5. In the old days, some would pay nurses with **victuals** so that they wouldn't be hungry.
   - ○ lodging
   - ○ food
   - ○ tools
   - ○ horses

6. Nurses often use a **sterilizer** to make sure their tools are free of germs and disease.
   - ○ machine that makes oxygen
   - ○ machine that makes tools
   - ○ machine that kills germs
   - ○ machine that operates

Unit 10, Lesson 2

Part 3: Using a Dictionary

A **dictionary** contains an alphabetical listing of words. Much information is provided about each word or **entry**. Dictionaries tell you how to pronounce a word, its part of speech, and its meaning. Dictionaries may also tell you the history of the word. It may also give synonyms, or words that mean almost the same thing. When you look up a word, use the context of what you are reading to help you choose the definition that makes the most sense.

A. In each of the sentences, one word is underlined. Find the word in the boxed dictionary entries below. Decide which meaning best matches the context, or ideas, in the sentence. Then write the part of speech and the definition on the lines provided.

<table>
<tr><td></td><td>**Part of Speech**</td><td>**Definition**</td></tr>
<tr><td>1. Allen wasn't sure he could <u>handle</u> watching his father in pain.</td><td>_____</td><td>_____</td></tr>
<tr><td>2. The nurse stuck the <u>needle</u> into his father's arm.</td><td>_____</td><td>_____</td></tr>
<tr><td>3. His father had been hurt riding down the <u>steep</u> mountainside</td><td>_____</td><td>_____</td></tr>
<tr><td>4. Friends carried Allen's father away on a <u>stretcher</u></td><td>_____</td><td>_____</td></tr>
<tr><td>5. It was not a good time to <u>needle</u> his father about the accident.</td><td>_____</td><td>_____</td></tr>
</table>

---

han•dle 1 (hăn′dl) *v.* **1.** To touch, lift, or hold with the hands. **2.** To deal or cope with — *n.* **2.** A part that is designed to be held.

nee•dle 1 (nēd′l) *n.* **1.** A small, pointed device used for sewing or in surgery — *v.* **1.** To prick or pierce with a needle. **2.** To tease or provoke someone.

steep 1 (stēp) *adj.* **1.** Having a sharp rise or incline. **2.** At a fast rate. **3.** A large amount, expensive.
steep 2. (stēp) *v.* To soak in liquid in order to clean.

stretch•er 1 (strĕch′ûr) *n.* **1.** A person that stretches something. **2.** A piece of cloth, usually canvas, spread across a wooden frame for the sick or wounded.

Unit 10, Lesson 3

Power Words Review

Look at the words below. Circle any that you think you may know. Be ready to tell the class what the word means. Also tell the class how you think you know that word.

arms	determined	hide	raging
brush	fair	implore	runaway
check	falsehood	intend	splint
count	famine	modest	steep
courage	grain	needle	sterilize
deed	handle	pole	stretcher

Part 1: Multiple-Meaning Words

The word *multiple* means many. **Multiple-meaning words** are words that have more than one meaning. For example, the word *play* can mean "to have fun." It can also be a dramatic production at a theater.

A. Fluency: Practice reading the paragraph below until you can read it smoothly. For each **bold** word, decide which definition from the bottom of the page best fits the way the word in used. Write the letter of the correct definition in the blank.

The young man had been standing in the **brush (1)** for hours. Ever since he had bought the castle and received his **deed (2)** he had been watching for robbers. He was careful to **check (3)** for them around sunset. He had heard that the thieves would **hide (4)** because they knew he carried **arms (5)**. Hopefully they'd stay away.

_____ 1. a. a device with bristles attached to a handle and used for painting
   b. to clean, polish, or scrub
   c. a thick growth of bushes and shrubs

_____ 2. a. an act or action
   b. a sealed document related to property

_____ 3. a. a quick stop or halt
   b. a bill at a restaurant
   c. to inspect in order to determine accuracy or quantity
   d. to try to stop another player in ice hockey

_____ 4. a. to put or keep out of sight
   b. to seek safety
   c. the skin of an animal

_____ 5. a. the upper limbs of the body
   b. weapons, especially firearms

Name _____ Date _____

Part 2: Context Clues

Remember that you can often figure out the meaning of an unknown word from the words that appear nearby. The words or phrases that surround an unknown word are called **context clues.**

A. Use context clues to figure out the meaning of the **bold** word. Darken in the circle with the correct definition.

1. I only got a **modest** salary for my work at the store.
   - ○ good
   - ○ large
   - ○ small
   - ○ worthless

2. Luis said that all day he had **intended** to go to the bank but never made it.
   - ○ not wanted
   - ○ planned
   - ○ decided
   - ○ run

3. The **splint** held the broken leg in place.
   - ○ shaft
   - ○ branch
   - ○ rope
   - ○ brace

4. Paul was **determined** about his making the track team this year.
   - ○ interested
   - ○ firm
   - ○ bored
   - ○ wanting

5. Many people starved to death during the great **famine**.
   - ○ shortage of food
   - ○ spread of disease
   - ○ spread of fire
   - ○ loss of water

6. We **implored** our math teacher not to give us homework over the holidays.
   - ○ demanded
   - ○ wished
   - ○ begged
   - ○ told

Unit 10, Lesson 3

Part 3: Using a Dictionary

A **dictionary** contains an alphabetical listing of words. Much information is provided about each word or **entry**. When you look up a word, use the context of what you are reading to help you choose the definition that makes the most sense.

A. In each of the sentences, one word is underlined. Find the word in the boxed dictionary entries below. Decide which meaning best matches the context, or ideas, in the sentence. Then write the part of speech and the definition on the lines provided.

	Part of Speech	Definition
1. Saul grabbed the <u>handle</u> of the shovel and went to work	_____	_____
2. I wouldn't believe his <u>story</u> about last night.	_____	_____
3. My father works on the seventh <u>story</u> of his office building	_____	_____
4. My aunt tried to <u>steep</u> her new dress in bleach to get the stain out.	_____	_____
5. Art loves to <u>hide</u> his toys from the other kids.	_____	_____

---

brush 1 (brŭsh) *n.* **1.** A device with bristles attached to a handle and used for painting.— *v.* **2.** To clean, polish, or scrub with a brush.
brush 2 (brŭsh) *n.* **1.** A thick growth of bushes and shrubs.

han•dle 1 (hăn′dl) *v.* **1.** To touch, lift, or hold with the hands. **2.** To deal or cope with — *n.* **1.** A part that is designed to be held.

hide 1 (hīd) *v.* **1.** To put or keep out of sight. **2.** To seek safety or refuge.
hide 2 (hīd) *n.* **1.** The skin of an animal.

steep 1 (stēp) *adj.* **1.** Having a sharp rise or incline. **2.** At a fast rate. **3.** A large amount, expensive.
steep 2 (stēp) *v.* **1.** To soak in liquid in order to clean.

sto•ry 1 (stôr′ē) *n.* **1.** An account of an event or series of events. **2.** A newspaper article. **3.** A lie.
sto•ry 2 (stôr′ē) *n.* **1.** A set of rooms on the same level of a building

Unit 10, Test

Part A: Multiple-Meaning Words

Directions: Read each sentence below. Find the word that fits in both sentences.

1. My dad thought to _____ around town during rush hour to avoid traffic.

   Teresa loved her new cotton _____ that she wore the first day of school.

   ○ hide
   ○ handle
   ○ skirt
   ○ head

2. I want to _____ my phone bill for errors.

   The restaurant's _____ was very expensive.

   ○ hide
   ○ fair
   ○ check
   ○ meal

3. The _____ for the new house was signed and sealed.

   That was a good _____ you did when you helped the older lady.

   ○ count
   ○ deed
   ○ check
   ○ painting

4. Ted checked his _____ to make sure he wasn't late.

   I love to _____ people shop at the mall.

   ○ arms
   ○ handle
   ○ count
   ○ watch

5. My _____ were tired after holding up the sign for an hour.

   The enemy had powerful _____ with which they were attacking.

   ○ splints
   ○ courage
   ○ arms
   ○ deed

Unit 10, Test

Part B: Context Clues

Directions: For each numbered blank, there is a list of words with the same number. Choose the word from each list that best completes the meaning of the paragraph.

1. The _____ was very brave. It took a lot of _____ to escape from the slave
   (1)   (2)
   owner and his mean men in the middle of the night.

   1. ○ count   2. ○ wealth
       ○ soldier   ○ courage
       ○ teacher   ○ love
       ○ runaway   ○ hate

2. I had _____ to tell the truth. However, the _____ just came out before I
   (3)   (4)
   realized I had lied.

   3. ○ counted   4. ○ courage
       ○ intended   ○ modesty
       ○ implored   ○ falsehood
       ○ deeded   ○ truth

3. The river was _____. My friend and I were _____ to ride the wild and
   (5)   (6)
   powerful water no matter who told us that we should not.

   5. ○ modest   6. ○ scared
       ○ calm   ○ afraid
       ○ raging   ○ determined
       ○ steep   ○ sad

4. The restaurant bill was very _____. I think my uncle was nice and generous
   (7)
   when he _____ us for ten minutes to let him pay it.
   (8)

   7. ○ modest   8. ○ questioned
       ○ steep   ○ implored
       ○ high   ○ handled
       ○ expensive   ○ counted

Unit 10, Test

Part C: Using a Dictionary

Directions: In each of the sentences, one word is underlined. Find the word in the boxed dictionary entries below. Decide which meaning best matches the context, or ideas, in the sentence. Write the part of speech and the definition on the lines provided.

	Part of Speech	Definition

1. Please be careful to <u>handle</u> the fragile glass very carefully.   _____   _____

2. The <u>hide</u> of a deer was used for clothing in the old days.   _____   _____

3. You will have to <u>brush</u> the floor very hard to get the dirt off.   _____   _____

4. The hill was too <u>steep</u> for us to ride our bikes up.   _____   _____

5. The sick man was carried to the hospital on a <u>stretcher</u>.   _____   _____

6. Dan told a <u>story</u> that wasn't true about us going to the fair.   _____   _____

---

brush 1 (brŭsh) *n.* **1.** A device with bristles attached to a handle and used for painting.— *v.* **2.** To clean, polish, or scrub with a brush.
brush 2 (brŭsh) *n.* **1.** A thick growth of bushes and shrubs.

han•dle 1 (hăn′dl) *v.* **1.** To touch, lift, or hold with the hands. **2.** To deal or cope with — *n.* **1.** A part that is designed to be held.

hide 1 (hīd) *v.* **1.** To put or keep out of sight. **2.** To seek safety or refuge.
hide 2 (hīd) *n.* **1.** The skin of an animal.

nee•dle 1 (nēd′dl) *n.* **1.** A small, pointed device used for sewing or in surgery — *v.* **1.** To prick or pierce with a needle. **2.** To tease someone

steep 1 (stēp) *adj.* **1.** Having a sharp rise or incline. **2.** At a fast rate. **3.** A large amount, expensive.
steep 2 (stēp) *v.* **1.** To soak in liquid in order to clean.

sto•ry 1 (stôr′ē) *n.* **1.** An account of an event or series of events. **2.** A newspaper article. **3.** A lie.
sto•ry 2 (stôr′ē) *n.* **1.** A set of rooms on the same level of a building

stretch•er 1 (strĕch′ûr) *n.* **1.** A person that stretched something. **2.** A piece of cloth, usually canvas, spread across a wooden frame for the sick or wounded.

Unit 11, Lesson 1

Power Words

Look at the words below. Circle any that you think you may know. Be ready to tell the class what the word means. Also tell the class how you think you know that word.

banned	biography	gait	reins
bibliography	biology	optician	role
bibliophile	chronological	public	waste

Part 1: Homophones

Remember that words that sound the same but have different spellings and meanings are called **homophones**. For example, **bear** and **bare** are homophones. Here are some other examples of homophones.

waist and **waste**   **when** and **win**   **wear** and **where**

rains and **reins**   **gate** and **gait**   **for** and **fore** and **four**

band and **banned**   **roll** and **role**   **to** and **two** and **too**

A. Each sentence has two homophones in parentheses. Circle the correct homophone that makes sense with the meaning of the sentence. Use a dictionary if necessary.

1. Roman gladiators were fighters who fought (four, fore, for) honor and glory.

2. These fighters would (where, wear) armor to protect themselves against the enemy.

3. Sometimes, they (band, banned) together and fought in groups.

4. Some gladiators rode horses in races, holding tightly to the (rains, reins).

5. The gladiators would also drive chariots pulled by (for, fore, four) horses.

6. The horses would pull chariots at a very fast (gait, gate).

7. Once in a while, a chariot would (role, roll) over.

8. A smart gladiator carried a knife or dagger at his (waist, waste).

9. He would be able (too, to, two) cut himself loose from the chariot if it crashed.

10. (Win, When) a gladiator was injured, the people would decide if he lived or died.

Unit 11, Lesson 1

Part 2: Greek and Latin Roots

Many English words are made up of word parts from other languages, especially Greek and Latin. These word parts are called **roots**. A root cannot stand alone, but knowing its meaning helps you figure out the meaning of the whole word. A group of words with the same root is called a **word family**. Study the chart of **Greek** roots below.

Root	Meaning	Example
bio	life	biography
chron	time	chronological
bibl, biblio	books	bibliophile
opt	visible	optical
cardi	heart	cardiac

A. Underline the root of each word in **Column A**. Then match each word with its correct meaning in **Column B**. Write the letter of the correct meaning in the space provided. Use a dictionary if necessary.

Column A

1. _____ optical

2. _____ biography

3. _____ cardiac arrest

4. _____ bibliography

5. _____ chronological

6. _____ biology

7. _____ optician

8. _____ cardiology

9. _____ bibliophile

10. _____ chronometer

Column B

A. the science of the structure of life

B. one who makes lens and eyeglasses

C. an extremely accurate clock

D. a heart attack that stops the heart beat

E. a list or books or writings

F. one who loves books

H. the study of the heart

G. having to do with the sight or vision

I. arranged in time order

J. a description of someone's life

Part 3: Syllabication

A **syllable** is a word part with one vowel sound. Remember that the vowels are the letters *a, e, i, o, u,* and sometimes *y*. All other letters are consonants. The chart below shows you the long and short vowel sounds.

Vowel	Long Sound	Short Sound
a	"a" as in day	"a" as in cat
e	"e" as in be	"e" as in set
i	"i" as in lie	"i" as in sit
o	"o" as in low	"o" as in hot
u	"u" as in blue	"u" as in bug

If you break an unknown word into syllables, it may help you figure out what the word means. Look at the rules below to see the correct places to divide words into syllables.

1. *war • plane* (between two words of a compound word)
2. *dis • arm* or *try • ing* (between a base word and a prefix or suffix)
3. *cor • rect* (between double consonants)
4. *clus • ter* (between two consonants, with vowels both before and after)
5. *be • hind* (<u>before</u> a single consonant if the vowel before it has a <u>long</u> sound)
6. *nev • er* (<u>after</u> a single consonant if the vowel before it has a <u>short</u> sound)

A. Use the rules above to divide each of the words below into its syllables. Write the syllables on the blanks provided. Then write which rule tells you how to divide a word.

Word	Syllables		Rule
1. winner	= _____	+ _____	_____
2. lightweight	= _____	+ _____	_____
3. cheering	= _____	+ _____	_____
4. decide	= _____	+ _____	_____
5. public	= _____	+ _____	_____
6. loudly	= _____	+ _____	_____
7. cabin	= _____	+ _____	_____

Unit 11, Lesson 2

Power Words

Look at the words below. Circle any that you think you may know. Be ready to tell the class what the word means. Also tell the class how you think you know that word.

audio	foul	junction	province
defect	fragment	manufacture	site
factory	gracious	mourn	wring

Part 1: Homophones

Remember that words that sound the same but have different spellings and meanings are called **homophones**. For example, **ball** and **bawl** are homophones. Here are some other examples of homophones.

foul and **fowl**	**cheap** and **cheep**	**mourn** and **morn**
sight and **site**	**oh** and **owe**	**ring** and **wring**
past and **passed**	**threw** and **through**	**born** and **borne**

A. Each sentence has two homophones in parentheses. Circle the correct homophone that makes sense with the meaning of the sentence. Use a dictionary if necessary.

1. In ancient Egypt, kings were (born, borne) into royal families.

2. In the (past, passed) these kings were buried in deep tombs.

3. The (site, sight) of the tomb was kept a great secret.

4. The people would (mourn, morn) the loss of their king.

5. Many people would (ball, bawl) at his death.

6. They would (ring, wring) their hands in sadness as his body was carried away.

7. The tombs were closed up and sometimes the air inside became (fowl, foul).

8. (Threw, Through) time the location of the tombs was forgotten.

9. Later scientists would ask rich people who weren't (cheap, cheep) to help them search for the tombs.

10. The rich do not worry about the money the scientists (owe, oh) them because they expect to get it back in treasure.

Name _____   Date _____

Part 2: Greek and Latin Roots

Many English words are made up of word parts from other languages, especially Greek and Latin. These word parts are called **roots**. A root cannot stand alone, but knowing its meaning helps you figure out the meaning of the whole word. A group of words with the same root is called a **word family**. Study the chart of **Latin** roots below.

Root	Meaning	Example
fract, frag	break	fragment
grat, grac	pleasing	gracious
fact, fect	do, make	factory
junct	join	junction
aud	hear	audio

A. Underline the root of each word in **Column A.** Then match each word with its correct meaning in **Column B.** Write the letter of the correct meaning in the space provided. Use a dictionary if necessary.

Column A

1. _____ junction

2. _____ gratify

3. _____ manufacture

4. _____ audio

5. _____ fragment

6. _____ defect

7. _____ factory

8. _____ audiotape

9. _____ conjunction

10. _____ gracious

Column B

A. something made wrong or improperly

B. related to sound

C. a broken-off piece

D. to please or sastify

E. a place where two things join

F. a place where things are made

G. a word that joins other words or phrases

H. kind and warm; pleasing

I. to make a raw material into a finished piece

J. a magnetic tape that records sound

Unit 11, Lesson 2

Part 3: Syllabication

A **syllable** is a word part with one vowel sound. If you break an unknown word into syllables, it may help you figure out what the word means. Look at the rules below to see the correct places to divide words into syllables. Remember that the vowels are the letters *a, e, i, o, u,* and sometimes *y.* All other letters are consonants.

1. *war • plane* (between two words of a compound word)
2. *dis • arm* or *quick • ly* (between a base word and a prefix or suffix)
3. *cor • rect* (between double consonants)
4. *clus • ter* (between two consonants, with vowels both before and after)
5. *be • hind* (<u>before</u> a single consonant if the vowel before it has a <u>long</u> sound)
6. *nev • er* (<u>after</u> a single consonant if the vowel before it has a <u>short</u> sound)

A. Write the syllables of the words below on the lines. Then on the third blank provided, write the number of the rule from above that tells you how to separate each word.

Word		Syllables	Rule
1. himself	=	_____ + _____	_____
2. million	=	_____ + _____	_____
3. almost	=	_____ + _____	_____
4. writer	=	_____ + _____	_____
5. graveyard	=	_____ + _____	_____
6. outdoors	=	_____ + _____	_____
7. seven	=	_____ + _____	_____
8. saddest	=	_____ + _____	_____
9. defend	=	_____ + _____	_____
10. bodies	=	_____ + _____	_____
11. slowly	=	_____ + _____	_____
12. province	=	_____ + _____	_____

Unit 11, Lesson 3

Power Words

Look at the words below. Circle any that you think you may know. Be ready to tell the class what the word means. Also tell the class how you think you know that word.

audio	chronological	gracious	public
banned	defect	junction	reins
bibliography	factory	manufacture	role
bibliophile	foul	mourn	site
biography	fragment	optician	waste
biology	gait	province	wring

Part 1: Homophones

Words that sound the same but have different spellings and meanings are called **homophones**. For example, **sail** and **sale** are homophones.

A. In the blank provided, write a homophone for each of the words below. Some words have two homophones. Use a dictionary if necessary.

1. foul _____

2. site _____

3. gait _____

4. reins _____

5. role _____

6. waste _____

7. banned _____

8. mourn _____

B. Fluency: Read the story below. There are 14 homophones in the following story; however, each of them is the wrong word. Circle the incorrect homophone and write the correct word above it. Then practice reading the story until you can read it smoothly.

Win John walked threw his house, he smelled a fowl odor. Wear is that odor coming from he wondered? He began to ring his hands as he past into the kitchen. He could not believe the site. A large amount of waist had come from the sink. He walked with a fast gate two the sink. He saw the problem. He had bought a cheep plug. Plugs like these should be band, even if he did only pay for cents. "Owe me," he sighed.

Unit 11, Lesson 3

Part 2: Greek and Latin Roots

Many English words are made up of word parts from other languages, especially Greek and Latin. These word parts are called **roots**. A root cannot stand alone, but knowing its meaning helps you figure out the meaning of the whole word. Study the chart of **Greek** and **Latin** roots below. Then do the exercise on this and the next page.

Root	Meaning	Example
bio	life	biography
chron	time	chronological
bibl, biblio	books	bibliophile
opt	visible	optical
cardi	heart	cardiac
fract, frag	break	fragment
grat, grac	pleasing	gracious
fact, fect	do, make	factory
junct	join	junction
aud	hear	audio

A. Match the root of each word in **Column A** with its correct meaning in **Column B**. Write the letter of the correct meaning in the space provided.

Column A

1. _____ optician
2. _____ conjunction
3. _____ cardiac arrest
4. _____ bibliography
5. _____ chronological
6. _____ biology

Column B

A. a word that joins other words or phrases
B. one who makes lens and eyeglasses
C. the science of the structure of life
D. a heart attack that stops the heart beat
E. arranged in time order
F. a list of books or writings

B. Underline the Greek or Latin root of each of the words in **Column A**.

1. junction
2. audiotape
3. gracious
4. gratify
5. fragment
6. cardiac
7. optical
8. defect
9. factory

Unit 11, Lesson 3

Part 3: Syllabication

A **syllable** is a word part with one vowel sound. Look at the rules below to see the correct places to divide words into syllables.

1. *war • plane* (between two words of a compound word)
2. *dis • arm* or *try • ing* (between a base word and a prefix or suffix)
3. *cor • rect* (between double consonants)
4. *clus • ter* (between two consonants, with vowels both before and after)
5. *be • hind* (<u>before</u> a single consonant if the vowel before it has a <u>long</u> sound)
6. *nev • er* (<u>after</u> a single consonant if the vowel before it has a <u>short</u> sound)

A. Use the rules above to divide each of the words below into its syllables. Write the syllables on the blanks provided. Then write which rule tells you how to divide a word.

Word	Syllables	Rule
1. million	= _____ + _____	_____
2. lightweight	= _____ + _____	_____
3. slowly	= _____ + _____	_____
4. decide	= _____ + _____	_____
5. public	= _____ + _____	_____
6. magic	= _____ + _____	_____
7. cabin	= _____ + _____	_____
8. almost	= _____ + _____	_____

Unit 11, Test

Part A: Homophones

Directions: Fill in the letter of the word that is a homophone of the **bold** word

1. **role**
   - Ⓐ rule
   - Ⓑ raol
   - Ⓒ roll
   - Ⓓ rold
   - Ⓔ roe

2. **site**
   - Ⓕ sit
   - Ⓖ sight
   - Ⓗ syte
   - Ⓘ sign
   - Ⓙ sigh

3. **foul**
   - Ⓚ fore
   - Ⓛ faul
   - Ⓜ fowl
   - Ⓝ fool
   - Ⓞ fell

4. **waste**
   - Ⓟ ways
   - Ⓠ wade
   - Ⓡ weigh
   - Ⓢ weird
   - Ⓣ waist

5. **gait**
   - Ⓐ gay
   - Ⓑ gate
   - Ⓒ game
   - Ⓓ gat
   - Ⓔ great

6. **mourn**
   - Ⓕ mort
   - Ⓖ murn
   - Ⓗ morn
   - Ⓘ morgue
   - Ⓙ morph

7. **wring**
   - Ⓚ wing
   - Ⓛ wreath
   - Ⓜ rang
   - Ⓝ ring
   - Ⓞ earring

8. **banned**
   - Ⓟ banter
   - Ⓠ bans
   - Ⓡ band
   - Ⓢ barn
   - Ⓣ bend

9. **reins**
   - Ⓐ ruins
   - Ⓑ reads
   - Ⓒ reds
   - Ⓓ rains
   - Ⓔ rests

10. **ball**
    - Ⓕ bald
    - Ⓖ bawl
    - Ⓗ bail
    - Ⓘ bale
    - Ⓙ bane

Unit 11, Test

Part B: Greek and Latin Roots

Directions: Match the meaning of the word in **Column B** with the word in **Column A**. Fill in the letter of the definition on the blank provided.

Column A

1. _____ bibliography
2. _____ factory
3. _____ audio
4. _____ optician
5. _____ conjunction
6. _____ junction
7. _____ defect
8. _____ cardiac arrest
9. _____ fragment
10. _____ chronological
11. _____ gracious
12. _____ biography

Column B

A. a word that joins other words or phrases
B. related to sound
C. a place where things are made
D. a heart attack that stops the heart beat
E. something made wrong or improperly
F. arranged in time order
G. kind and warm; pleasing
H. a description of someone's life
I. a small, broken off piece
J. one who makes lens and eyeglasses
K. a place where two things join
L. a list or books or writings

Directions: Each Latin and Greek root below has two definitions. Only one is correct. Write the letter of the correct one on the blank provided.

1. _____ bio   A. life   B. heart
2. _____ fact, fect   A. do, make   B. join
3. _____ chron   A. break   B. time
4. _____ junct   A. join   B. books
5. _____ bibl, biblio A. visible   B. books
6. _____ opt   A. pleasing   B. visible
7. _____ grat, grac   A. heart   B. pleasing
8. _____ cardi   A. join   B. heart

Unit 11, Test

Part C: Syllabication

Directions: Separate the following words into syllables. Write the syllables on the lines.

1. outdoors = _____ + _____

2. slowly = _____ + _____

3. fragment = _____ + _____

4. decide = _____ + _____

5. million = _____ + _____

6. optical = _____ + _____ + _____

7. lightweight = _____ + _____ + _____

8. cabin = _____ + _____

9. writer = _____ + _____

10. loudly = _____ + _____

11. factory = _____ + _____ + _____

12. seven = _____ + _____

13. saddest = _____ + _____

14. baseball = _____ + _____

15. bodies = _____ + _____

16. almost = _____ + _____

17. gratify = _____ + _____ + _____

18. himself = _____ + _____

19. province = _____ + _____

20. public = _____ + _____

Unit 12, Lesson 1

Power Words

Look at the words below. Circle any that you think you may know. Be ready to tell the class what the word means. Also tell the class how you think you know that word.

automatic	foreigner	horror	secretly
double-cross	frantic	plot	tantrum
estate	global	seaward	typical

Part 1: Idioms

An **idiom** is a statement or phrase that doesn't mean exactly what the words say. People in different places have different ways of saying things. For example, to say that a person "has a green thumb" does not mean that his thumb is the color green. It means that this person is able to grow plants very easily. "Has a green thumb" is an idiom.

A. Each sentence below has an underlined idiom. Use the words around the idiom to help you figure out what the idiom means. Then read the list of definitions below. Write the letter of the definition that matches the idiom in the line behind the sentence.

A. to separate from others   F. to be removed from a group
B. very good   G. to watch someone carefully
C. acting wild or very excited   H. to try as hard as one can
D. to understand   I. running right behind someone
E. going very fast   J. relax

1. Jason ran track so well at school that he would never be <u>cut from</u> the team. _____

2. He liked track because he once saw the crowd <u>going bananas</u> at a meet. _____

3. He thought it would be <u>peaches and cream</u> if he won his first race. _____

4. His coach had his <u>eye on him</u> hoping he would be a great runner. _____

5. At practice before the meet, Jason decided to <u>take it easy</u>. _____

6. The other members of the track team were going <u>all out</u>. _____

7. The coach told Jason he better be <u>smoking</u> in the actual race. _____

8. It <u>came to</u> Jason that he better try hard. _____

9. When the gun went off, the other runners were <u>nipping at his heels</u>. _____

10. On the last lap, however, Jason was able to <u>break free</u> and win the race. _____

Unit 12, Lesson 1

Part 2: Context Clues

When you come to a word that you don't know, read the words near the unknown word carefully. These words may give you **context clues** that help you figure out what the unknown word means. For example, in the sentences below you see that the definition of *annoy* means "to bother or upset."

> Maria really annoys me with her constant yelling and crying.

A. Use context clues to figure out the definition of each **boldfaced** word.

1. Helen would often have **tantrums.** She would suddenly get violent and very angry.

   Tantrum means _____

2. Other people would watch with **horror,** disgusted at the terrible way Helen behaved.

   Horror means _____

3. When Helen was angry, she would **rant** very loudly at others like a wild animal.

   Rant means _____

4. Helen's family lived on a small **estate,** a large house surrounded by a lot of land.

   Estate means _____

5. One day a **foreigner** arrived to try to help Helen. Helen did not like this person from another country.

   Foreigner means _____

6. Helen thought her parents must have thought up a **plot,** or secret plan, to get her to behave.

   Plot means _____

7. Helen was sure her parents were trying to **double-cross** her. She didn't like to be tricked.

   Double-cross means _____

8. Helen would finally learn to **mind** her parents. She would behave and do whatever they told her to.

   Mind means _____

Name _____   Date _____

Part 3: Structural Analysis

A **base word** is a word that can stand alone. A **suffix** is a word part added to the ending of a base word. The following suffixes change a base word into an adverb. An adverb answers the questions *how, where, when,* or *to what extent.*

Base	Suffix	Examples
slow	**-ly**	slow<u>ly</u>
sky	**-ward**	sky<u>ward</u>
happy	**-ily**	happ<u>ily</u>
clock	**-wise**	clock<u>wise</u>
music	**-ally**	music<u>ally</u>

A. Add the correct ending to the following base words to make them adverbs. In some instances, you may need to change a **y** to an **i.** Write the new word on the blank.

1. quick: _____

2. to: _____

3. day: _____

4. secret: _____

5. global: _____

6. length: _____

7. automatic: _____

8. sleep: _____

9. crazy: _____

10. typical: _____

11. frantic: _____

12. sea: _____

Unit 12, Lesson 2

Power Words

Look at the words below. Circle any that you think you may know. Be ready to tell the class what the word means. Also tell the class how you think you know that word.

auction	consequently	engineer	mountaineer
bulletin	counselor	inspect	occupy
commandant	dietician	machinist	utterance

Part 1: Idioms

Remember that an **idiom** is a statement or phrase that doesn't mean exactly what the words say. People in different places have different ways of saying things. For example, to say that a man is "cool as a cucumber" does not mean that he is cold or a vegetable. It means that this person is a neat person. "Cool as a cucumber" is an idiom.

A. Each sentence below has an underlined idiom. Use the words around the idiom to help you figure out what the idiom means. Then read the list of definitions below. Write the letter of the definition that matches the idiom in the line behind the sentence.

A. to survive
B. to pay attention to
C. in trouble
D. someone who isn't good
E. searched

F. to be brave
G. crazy
H. very popular
I. finally; eventually
G. just barely

1. Charles Lindbergh was <u>a big hit</u> when he flew across the Atlantic Ocean. _____

2. Many people thought he was <u>off his rocker</u> to do something so dangerous. _____

3. Lindbergh was able <u>to get by</u> on the money he made from his fame. _____

4. However, one night <u>a bad apple</u> kidnapped Lindbergh's baby. _____

5. Lindbergh had heard a noise upstairs but didn't <u>pay it any mind</u>. _____

6. Whoever had stolen his child was really <u>in the dog house</u>. _____

7. The police <u>combed the bushes</u> for any sign of the Lindbergh child. _____

8. The kidnapper had escaped <u>by the skin of his teeth</u>. _____

9. The Lindbergh family tried <u>to keep a stiff upper lip</u> during the ordeal. _____

10. <u>In the long run</u> the police were able to catch the kidnapper. _____

Unit 12, Lesson 2

Part 2: Context Clues

When you come to a word that you don't know, read the words near the unknown word carefully. These words may give you **context clues** that help you figure out what the unknown word means. For example, in the sentences below you see that the definition of *diplomatic* means "able to get along with many different people."

Chuck is so diplomatic. He knows the right thing to say so that no one gets mad.

A. Use context clues to figure out the definition of each **boldfaced** word.

1. The boy threw a hard, round **pellet** at the window and broke it.

   Pellet means _____

2. The sofa was covered with **lint** from the cat and dog who were losing their hair.

   Lint means _____

3. It was a hot day and a **gnat** was flying in our faces and annoying us.

   Gnat means_____

4. The porch was covered in ice; **consequently,** the boy slipped and fell down.

   Consequently means _____

5. When the policeman grabbed the thief by the hair, a small **tuft** of hair came out.

   Tuft means _____

6. The principal wrote a **bulletin** to announce the new cafeteria rules.

   Bulletin means_____

7. In a course in **physics** one studies the scientific laws of how things work.

   Physics means _____

8. The dying man's final **utterance** was so soft we couldn't understand what he said.

   Utterance means _____

Name _____ Date _____

Part 3: Structural Analysis

A **base word** is a word that can stand alone. A **suffix** is a word part added to the ending of a base word. The following suffixes change a base word into a noun that refers to someone who does something. Sometimes the spelling of the base word changes when adding one of these suffixes.

Base Word	Suffix	Examples
teach	-er	teach<u>er</u>
command	-ant	command<u>ant</u>
counsel	-or	counsel<u>or</u>
diet	-ician	diet<u>ician</u>
mountain	-eer	mountain<u>eer</u>
science	-ist	scient<u>ist</u>

A. Add an ending to the following base words to make them refer to persons. You may need to change the spelling of the base word. Write the new word on the blank.

1. play: _____

2. machine: _____

3. occupy: _____

4. engine: _____

5. beauty: _____

6. inspect: _____

7. race: _____

8. build: _____

9. auction: _____

10. conduct: _____

11. mathematics: _____

12. geology: _____

Unit 12, Lesson 3

Power Words Review

Look at the words below. Circle any that you think you may know. Be ready to tell the class what the word means. Also tell the class how you think you know that word.

auction	dietician	global	plot
automatic	double-cross	horror	seaward
bulletin	engineer	inspect	secretly
commandant	estate	machinist	tantrum
consequently	foreigner	mountaineer	typical
counselor	frantic	occupy	utterance

Part 1: Idioms

Remember that an **idiom** is a phrase that doesn't mean exactly what the words say.

A. Match the idiom in **Column A** with its meaning in **Column B**. Write the letter of the correct definition in the blank provided.

Column A

1. _____ a big hit
2. _____ off his rocker
3. _____ take it easy
4. _____ nipping at one's heels
5. _____ by the skin of one's teeth
6. _____ in the dog house
7. _____ combed the bushes
8. _____ cut from

Column B

A. crazy

B. in trouble

C. just barely

D. relax

E. running right behind someone

F. very popular

G. to be removed from a group; let go

H. searched

B. Fluency: Practice reading the following paragraph until you can read it smoothly. Then underline the seven idioms within it.

My cousin is just a bad apple. He's always getting into trouble. He'll start going bananas and do something stupid. I try not to pay him any mind. I tell him to take it easy. He's always in the dog house with his parents. The police have their eye on him. In the long run, he's going to get into big trouble if he doesn't change.

Unit 12, Lesson 3

Part 2: Context Clues

Remember that you can often figure out the meaning of an unknown word from the words that appear nearby. The words or phrases that surround an unknown word are called **context clues.**

A. Use context clues to figure out the meaning of the **bold** word. Darken in the circle with the correct definition.

1. The teacher read a **bulletin** to the class about the hours of the upcoming school fair.
   - ○ contract
   - ○ announcement
   - ○ novel
   - ○ letter

2. The wealthy family lived on a large **estate.**
   - ○ cabin with a garden
   - ○ mobile home with a yard
   - ○ grand home with a lot of land
   - ○ big boat

3. The teacher said that was the last **utterance** she would hear out of our talkative group.
   - ○ lie
   - ○ something said
   - ○ cough
   - ○ song

4. Sara **double-crosses** her brother by telling him to look away. Then she steals his candy.
   - ○ attacks
   - ○ loves
   - ○ takes care of
   - ○ tricks

5. My uncle is a **foreigner.** He is visiting from Sweden.
   - ○ eskimo
   - ○ someone from another city
   - ○ someone from another country
   - ○ vegetarian

6. When David's sister has a **tantrum,** she gets mad and screams for hours.
   - ○ angry reaction
   - ○ walk
   - ○ party
   - ○ birthday

Name _____   Date _____

Part 3: Structural Analysis

A **base word** is a word that can stand alone. A **suffix** is a word part added to the ending of a base word. Study the chart of suffixes below.

Base Word	Suffix	Examples
slow	-ly	slowly
sky	-ward	skyward
happy	-ily	happily
clock	-wise	clockwise
music	-ally	musically
teach	-er	teacher
command	-ant	commandant
counsel	-or	counselor
diet	-ician	dietician
mountain	-eer	mountaineer
science	-ist	scientist

A. Match the word in **Column A** with its meaning in **Column B.**

Column A

1. _____ automatically
2. _____ commandant
3. _____ globally
4. _____ occupant
5. _____ seaward
6. _____ auctioneer
7. _____ machinist
8. _____ dietician
9. _____ frantically
10. _____ counselor

Column B

A. towards the ocean

B. someone who understands nutrition

C. having to do with the entire earth

D. someone who gives advice

E. someone who works on machines

F. something that happens without help

G. someone who is a leader of a group

H. acting in an excited or crazy manner

I. someone who lives in a building

J. someone who accepts bids at an auction

Unit 12, Test

Part A: Idioms

Directions: Match the idiom in **Column A** with its meaning in **Column B.** Write the letter of the correct definition in the blank provided.

Column A	Column B
1. _____ off his rocker	A. going very fast
2. _____ smoking	B. crazy
3. _____ take it easy	C. just barely
4. _____ a bad apple	D. eventually; finally
5. _____ in the dog house	E. searched
6. _____ nipping at his heels	F. someone who isn't good
7. _____ has his eye on him	G. very popular
8. _____ a big hit	H. to be brave
9. _____ peaches and cream	I. acting wild or very excited
10. _____ cut from	J. relax
11. _____ keep a stiff upper lip	K. removed from a group, such as a team
12. _____ combed the bushes	L. in trouble
13. _____ in the long run	M. very good
14. _____ by the skin of his teeth	N. running right behind someone
15. _____ going bananas	O. to watch someone closely

Unit 12, Test

Part B: Context Clues

Directions: For each numbered blank, there is a list of words with the same number. Choose the word from each list that best completes the meaning of the paragraph.

1. Sasha is a _____. When she speaks, her _____ have a beautiful accent.
   (1)   (2)

   1. ○ counselor   2. ○ tantrum
       ○ dietician   ○ plot
       ○ foreigner   ○ utterances
       ○ engineer   ○ will power

2. Melissa had such a _____. When she found out her best friend had _____
   (3)   (4)
   her and taken her money she yelled and screamed for hours.

   3. ○ estate   4. ○ inspected
       ○ tantrum   ○ occupied
       ○ utterance   ○ double-crossed
       ○ auction   ○ auctioned

3. We read the notice in a _____. The rich family was moving and selling every
   (5)
   part of their huge _____.
   (6)

   5. ○ plot   6. ○ estate
       ○ bulletin   ○ plot
       ○ utterance   ○ auction
       ○ command   ○ global

4. Dan sat in _____ after he discovered the _____ to get rid of him. He
   (7)   (8)
   couldn't believe someone would do something so disgusting.

   7. ○ frantic   8. ○ counselor
       ○ secretly   ○ foreigner
       ○ horror   ○ estate
       ○ tantrum   ○ plot

Unit 12, Test

Part C: Structural Analysis

Directions: Use the clues below to fill in the answers of the crossword puzzle. Each answer is one of your Power Words.

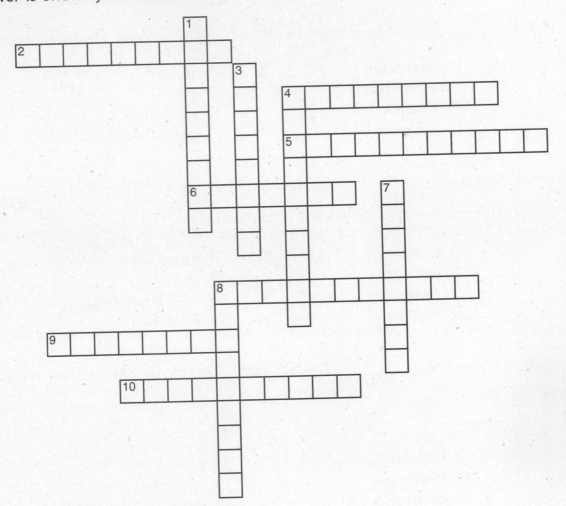

Across

2. someone who understands nutrition
4. someone who gives advice
5. someone who climbs mountains
6. towards the ocean
8. acting in an excited manner
9. someone who operates an engine
10. someone runs an auction

Down

1. someone who works on machines
3. someone who lives in a building
4. someone who is a leader
7. having to do with the entire earth
8. someone from another country

Answer Keys

Unit 1, Lesson 1

Part 1: Synonyms

A. 1. wonderful
2. hungry
3. stopped
4. difficulty
5. terrible

Part 2: Prefixes and Base Words

A. 1. un / equal – not the same or equal
2. re / play – to play again
3. pre / view – to view before others
4. un / able – not able
5. re / try – to try again
6. pre / shrunk – shrunk ahead of time
7. un / fair – not fair and just
8. re / took – to take again
9 pre / test – a test given before another test
10. un / bound – not tied or held down

B. 1. recount
2. unconscious
3. preschool
4. repossess
5. uncertain

Part 3: Compound Words

A. 1. sorehead
2. flashlight
3. dustpan
4. basketball
5. pullover

B. 1. flashlight
2. pullover
3. sorehead
4. basketball
5. dustpan
6. sorehead
7. basketball
8. dustpan
9. flashlight
10. pullover

Unit 1, Lesson 2

Part 1: Synonyms

A. 1. fooled
2. idea
3. fresh
4. imaginary
5. stepped

Part 2: Prefixes and Base Words

A. 1. comfort/able – pleasing
2. joy/ful – full of happiness
3. breath/less – exhausted, out of breath
4. truth/ful – one who tells the truth
5. price/less – very costly
6. move/able – able to be moved
7. fear/ful – scared or frightened
8. end/less – without stop or end
9. sustain/able – able to be kept as it is
10. thought/ful – one who thinks about others

B. 1. agreeable
2. youthful
3. painless
4. replaceable
5. lawful

Part 3: Compound Words

A. 1. jailbreak – to escape from jail
2. groundout – to hit a ball on the ground in baseball and be called out
3. overspend – to spend more than one has alloted
4. pinprick – a tiny puncture
5. scarecrow – a straw figure used in fields to frighten birds
6. stinkbug – an insect that emits a bad odor
7. crashworthy – something that holds up well in an accident
8. lawman – a policeman
9. sandcastle – a structure made of sand erected on beaches
10. underdog – one who is not expected to win

B. 1. grandmother
2. joyful
3. skateboard
4. truthful
5. lawful
6. crashworthy
7. fearful
8. overspend
9. comfortable
10. youthful
11. painless
12. thoughtful
13. agreeable
14. careful

Unit 1, Lesson 3

Part 1: Synonyms

A. 1. trouble
2. ravenous
3. deceived
4. froze
5. original
6. ghastly
7. mythical
8. splendid
9. tread
10. notion

Part 2: Prefixes and Suffixes

A. 1. D
    2. G
    3. A
    4. J
    5. H
    6. I
    7. F
    8. B
    9. C
    10. E

B. 1. preshrunk
    2. riceless
    3. unequal
    4. replay
    5. sustainable
    6. truthful

Part 3: Compound Words

```
O V E R S P E N D B P W G U +
+ + + + + + D + T A I O U N +
+ + + + + U + U + S N R B D +
+ + + + S + O + A K P C K E +
C + + T + D + N + E R E N R +
+ R P + N + D L + T I R I D +
K A A U + C + + + B C A T O +
N A O S A + + + + A K C S G +
+ R E S H T H G I L H S A L F
G + T R + W + + + L + + + + +
+ L + + B + O D A E H E R O S
E + + + + L + R + N A M W A L
+ + + + + + I + T + + + + + +
+ + + + + + + A + H + + + + +
P U L L O V E R J + Y + + + +
```

(Over,Down,Direction)
BASKETBALL(10,1,S)
CRASHWORTHY(1,5,SE)
DUSTPAN(7,2,SW)
FLASHLIGHT(15,9,W)
GROUNDOUT(1,10,NE)
JAILBREAK(9,15,NW)
LAWMAN(15,12,W)
OVERSPEND(1,1,E)
PINPRICK(11,1,S)
PULLOVER(1,15,E)
SANDCASTLE(10,3,SW)
SCARECROW(12,9,N)
SOREHEAD(15,11,W)
STINKBUG(13,8,N)
UNDERDOG(14,1,S)

Unit 1 Test

Part A: Synonyms

1. hungry
2. fresh
3. imaginary
4. stopped
5. terrible
6. idea
7. difficulty
8. wonderful
9. fooled
10. step

Part B: Prefixes and Suffixes

1. d
2. h
3. o
4. p
5. b
6. f
7. o
8. r
9. e
10. i

Part C: Compound Words

1. M
2. G
3. N
4. O
5. L
6. I
7. C
8. B
9. F
10. D
11. K
12. J
13. E
14. A
15. H

Unit 2, Lesson 1

Part 1: Synonyms

A. 1. moist
2. crept
3. barren
4. tardy
5. dim

Part 2: Homophones

A. 1. break
2. pale
3. red
4. maize
5. hoarse
6. heal
7. no
8. lead
9. night
10. flew

B. 1. rose – a type of flower: rows – a series of objects; a continuous line.
2. peek – a quick glance: peak – the highest point
3. seller – a person selling goods: cellar – a basement

Part 3: Structural Analysis

A. 1. sliding
2. doors
3. quickly
4. dreams
5. urgently
6. seas
7. burning
8. canyons
9. vertically
10. racing

B. Answers will vary for both pictures.
Possible answers for the dog: barking, yelping, snapping, biting, sleeping
Possible answers for the people: loudly, quietly, quickly, softly, nicely

Unit 2, Lesson 2

Part 1: Antonyms

A. 1. A
2. S
3. A
4. A
5. S
6. A
7. S
8. S
9. A
10. A

B. Answers will vary.
Possible answers include the following:
1. scream, yell
2. rising, growing
3. polite, nice
4. safety, security
5. fertile, rich
6. idiot, moron

Part 2: Homophones

A. 1. hi – a greeting of welcome: high – tall, lofty.
2. we'll – we will: wheel – a solid disk that turns around an axle
3. soar – to fly: sore – painful
4. knead – to mix with the hands: need – a lack of something
5. medal – a piece of metal stamped with a design: metal – an alloy of two or more metallic elements
6. night – period between sunrise and sunset: knight – a medieval gentleman
7. their – the possessive form of they: they're – they are: there – in that place
8. not – in no way: knot – an entanglement of rope, ribbon, or cord
9. rode – past tense of ride: rowed – to pull the oars of a boat to propel a boat: road – a paved way used for vehicles
10. made – past tense of make: maid – a woman servant

Part 3: Structural Analysis

A. 1. teacher
2. roared
3. boxes
4. missed
5. inspector
6. reader
7. lunches
8. passed
9. cashed
10. dancer

B.
1.	crashes	crashed	crasher
2.	kisses	kissed	kisser
3.	slaps	slapped	slapper
4.	brushes	brushed	brusher
5.	bombs	bombed	bomber

Unit 2, Lesson 3

Part 1: Antonyms

Answers may vary. Possible answers are as follows:

A. 1. child
2. obey
3. whisper
4. cellar
5. there
6. late, tardy
7. imperfect
8. smart, intelligent
9. wet, moist
10. vertically
11. dim
12. walked, crept

Part 2: Homophones

A. 1. soar
2. we'll
3. lead
4. hoarse
5. break
6. know
7. throne
8. maid
9. they're, there
10. heel
11. metal
12. rode, rowed

B. Correct homophones are as follows:

1. tale
2. flu
3. led
4. not
5. road
6. maize
7. made
8. we'll
9. no
10. sore
11. know
12. break
13. bear
14. waited
15. heal
16. our
17. medal
18. red

Part 3: Structural Analysis

A.
1. beaches
2. loudly
3. inspector
4. racing
5. reader
6. waited
7. toys
8. burning
9. quickly
10. boxes
11. dancer
12. lunches

Unit 2 Test

Part A: Antonyms

1. moist
2. shout
3. early
4. revolt
5. barren
6. dim
7. adult
8. safety
9. dummy
10. bad

Part B: Homophones

1. c. read
2. i. break
3. o. flew
4. p. need
5. d. metal
6. g. rowed
7. k. heel
8. q. throne
9. e. we'll
10. h. hoarse

Part C: Structural Analysis

1. doors
2. quickly
3. riding
4. walked
5. teacher
6. beaches
7. vertically
8. missed
9. roaring
10. dancer
11. canyons
12. urgently
13. inspector
14. lunches
15. sliding
16. cashed
17. loudly
18. burning
19. boxes
20. brushes

Unit 3, Lesson 1

Part 1: Compound Words

A.
1. smokestack – a vertical pipe through which gases are discharged
2. dockhand – a person who works on shipping docks
3. seashore – the area of land adjacent to the ocean
4. sailboat – a vessel powered by wind and sails
5. shipwreck – a vessel that has been sunk
6. boatload – a load of cargo on a boat

B.
1. sailboat
2. smokestack
3. seashore
4. shipwreck
5. dockhand
6. boatload

Part 2: Context Clues

A.
1. a hole at the top of a volcano
2. a person who studies volcanoes
3. the tube from the center of the volcano through which hot rock flows
4. rock that has become liquid from intense heat
5. burned up

B. Answers may vary. Accept answers in which sentences give a definition.

Part 3: Synonyms

A.
1. chance
2. beating
3. facts
4. scares
5. storm

B.
thrill – excite
burst – explode
search – explore
increase – expand
trade – exchange

Unit 3, Lesson 2

Part 1: Compound Words

A. 1. sun light – the light from the sun; daylight
   2. week end – Friday, Saturday, and Sunday
   3. fire works – explosive devices used at celebratory events
   4. under ground – below the surface of the earth
   5. water tight – an area that doesn't leak; resists water
   6. with stand – to put up with or endure
   7. sea men – sailors, people who work at sea

B. 1. underground   4. sunlight
   2. watertight   5. fireworks
   3. withstand

Part 2: Context Clues

A. 1. a weatherman
   2. a large body of floating ice
   3. earthquakes
   4. floods
   5. eruption

B. Answers may vary. Possible answers include:
   seaman – sailor
   vessel – ship, boat
   journey – trip
   storm – tempest
   rain – precipitation, shower
   navigate – steer
   frightened – scared
   risk – chance
   information – facts, data
   meteorologist – weatherman

Part 3: Synonyms

A. 1. searched   4. threat
   2. failure   5. benefit
   3. money   6. trip

Unit 3, Lesson 3

Part 1: Compound Words

A. 1. smokestack – funnel from the ship
   2. boatload – cargo on the ship's deck
   3. seaman – sailor on the back of the ship
   4. sunlight – below the sun
   5. sailboat – small boat behind the ship
   6. lifeboat – small boat on the ship's side
   7. seashore – land behind the ship
   8. motorcycle – two-wheeled vehicle on land
   9. dockhand – man standing on the dock
   10. shipwreck – broken ship below water

Part 2: Context Clues

A. 1. explode   6. disasters
   2. crater   7. volcanologists
   3. melted   8. tremor
   4. burned   9. spurting
   5. tube   10. meteorologists

Part 3: Synonyms

Across
   3. frightens
   8. currency
   10. malfunction
   11. sought

Down
   1. menace
   2. striking
   4. information
   5. outing
   6. tempest
   7. profit
   9. risk

Unit 3, Unit Test

Part A: Compound Words

1. C
2. F
3. I
4. G
5. K
6. D
7. N
8. L
9. O
10. M
11. A
12. H
13. J
14. B
15. E

1. A
2. B
3. A
4. B

Part B: Context Clues

1. volcanologist
2. crater
3. discharge
4. incinerate
5. meteorologist
6. deluge
7. molten
8. conduit

Part C: Synonyms

1. c
2. g
3. n
4. p
5. e
6. g
7. m
8. q
9. a
10. i

Unit 4, Lesson 1

Part 1: Compound Words

A. 1. birthday
2. hitchhike
3. newman
4. earthquake
5. offstage

B. 1. birthday
2. offstage
3. hitchhike
4. newsman
5. earthquake

Part 2: Greek and Latin Roots

A. 1. F   6. K
2. G   7. J
3. E   8. H
4. A   9. B
5. D   10. C

Part 3: Shades of Meaning

A. 1. D
2. B
3. C
4. B

Unit 4, Lesson 2

Part 1: Compound Words

A. 1. check out – to pay at the end of a hotel stay
2. gear shift – the lever used to change gears on a machine
3. drift wood – old wood that has floated in water for a long time
4. slip knot – a knot that pulls easily apart
5. rain wear – any piece of clothing made to wear in the rain

Part 2: Greek and Latin Roots

A. 1. B   6. A
2. H   7. G
3. E   8. C
4. K   9. F
5. J   10. D

Part 3: Shades of Meaning

A. 1. C
2. B
3. A
4. B

Unit 4, Lesson 3

Part 1: Compound Words

```
E Y + + + + + + H D + + S + +
+ A A + + + + + I E R + + L + +
+ + R D + + T G + I + + I + +
+ + + T H C A + + F + + P + +
+ + + + H T + + + T + T K + +
+ + + H S Q R + + W + U N + +
+ + I F + + U I + O + O O + +
+ K F + + + + A B O + K T + +
E O + + + + + + K D + C + + +
+ + T F I H S R A E G E + + +
N A M S W E N + + + + H + + +
+ + + + + + + + + + C + + +
+ + + + + + + + + + + + + +
+ + + R A I N W E A R + + + +
+ + + + + + + + + + + + + +
```

Part 2: Greek and Latin Roots

A.
1. B
2. G
3. E
4. A
5. D
6. H
7. C
8. F

Part 3: Shades of Meaning

A.
1. D
2. B
3. A
4. D

Unit 4, Unit Test

Part A: Compound Words

1. C
2. D
3. K
4. H
5. I
6. A
7. J
8. B
9. F
10. G
11. E
1. B
2. B
3. B
4. B

Part B: Greek and Latin Roots

1. A
2. J
3. L
4. B
5. H
6. M
7. F
8. K
9. D
10. G
11. O
12. N
13. E
14. I
15. C

1. B
2. A
3. B
4. A

Part C: Shades of Meaning

1. C
2. A
3. D
4. C
5. D

Unit 5, Lesson 1

Part 1: Prefixes and Base Words

A. 1. in/active – not active
    2. mis/read – to read incorrectly
    3. il/legal – unlawful
    4. dis/appear – to vanish
    5. in/operative – not working
    6. mis/understand – to not understand
    7. im/probable – not likely
    8. dis/agree – to not agree
    9. il/literate – unable to read
    10. mis/manage – to manage wrongly
    11. in/consistent – not steady or constant
    12. dis/arm – to take away weapons

Part 2: Context Clues

A. 1. angrily
    2. bad; evil
    3. know
    4. in an angry way
    5. calm
    6. recollections

Part 3: Syllabication

A. 1. cross + ly   2
    2. sum + mer   3
    3. mis + read   2
    4. prof + it   6
    5. up + stairs   1
    6. win + dow   4
    7. wi + der   5
    8. mag + ic   6
    9. fence + post   1
    10. snug + gle   3

B. 1. information
    2. replanted
    3. misfortune
    4. distress
    5. profit
    6. shortage
    7. impatiently

Unit 5, Lesson 2

Part 1: Suffixes and Base Words

A. 1. loud/er – more loud
    2. tempt/ation – something that tempts one
    3. amaze/ment – the state of being amazed
    4. grand/est – the most grand or wonderful
    5. participa/tion – to take part
    6. weak/er – more weak
    7. wonder/ment – a state of wonder or awe
    8. silli/est – the most silly
    9. recogni/tion – a state of knowing or recognizing
    10. encourage/ment – a state of providing support
    11. inspect/ion – a state of being inspected
    12. amuse/ment – a state of being amused

Part 2: Context Clues

A. 1. race
    2. fit the requirements
    3. wide street
    4. feel sorrow
    5. sent off
    6. made steady

Part 3: Syllabication

A. 1. grand + est   2
    2. dres + ser   3
    3. pho + to   5
    4. girl + friend   1
    5. mod + el   6
    6. dis + patch   2
    7. jac + ket   4
    8. be + fore   5
    9. din + ner   3
    10. in + side   1
    11. weak + er   2
    12. sec + ond   6

B. 1. inspection
    2. qualify
    3. grandest
    4. boulevard
    5. sadder
    6. weaker
    7. amusement

Unit 5, Lesson 3

Part 1: Affixes and Base Words

A.
1. J
2. D
3. H
4. I
5. B
6. E
7. A
8. G
9. C
10. F

Part 2: Context Clues

A.
1. fit the requirements
2. bad; evil
3. feel sorrow
4. in an angry way
5. sent off
6. recollections

Part 3: Syllabication

A.
1. dis + arm
2. grand + est
3. sum + mer
4. jac + ket
5. girl + friend
6. mag + ic
7. dis + patch
8. dis + ap + pear
9. re + as + sure
10. il + le + gal

B.
1. sadder – 2
2. mismanage – 3
3. grandest – 2
4. reassure – 3
5. weaker – 2
6. illegal – 3
7. wicked – 2
8. recognize – 3
9. boulevard – 3
10. inspection – 3
11. amazement - 3

Unit 5, Unit Test

Part A: Affixes and Base Words

1. e
2. f
3. m
4. s
5. b
6. i
7. l
8. r
9. a
10. h

Part B: Context Clues

1. grieve
2. memories
3. braced
4. boulevard
5. wicked
6. crossly
7. marathon
8. qualify

Part C: Syllabication

1. sad + der
2. dis + patch
3. mag + ic
4. girl + friend
5. a + maze + ment
6. weak + er
7. in + spec + tion
8. a + muse + ment
9. grand + est
10. jac + ket
11. mis + read
12. dis + arm
13. il + le + gal
14. mis + man + age
15. in + ac + tive
16. dis + a + gree
17. dis + ap + pear
18. wick + ed
19. re + as + sure
20. sum + mer

Unit 6, Lesson 1

Part 1: Idioms

A.
1. F
2. G
3. B
4. G
5. H

6. I
7. C
8. D
9. E
10. A

Part 2: Synonyms

A.
1. private
2. look
3. disturb

4. liking
5. talking
6. spun

Part 3: Multiple Meaning Words

A.
1. b
2. a
3. a
4. c

5. b
6. b
7. b
8. b

Unit 6, Lesson 2

Part 1: Idioms

A.
1. D
2. I
3. A
4. H
5. B

6. C
7. G
8. F
9. J
10. E

Part 2: Synonyms

A.
1. tangled
2. spoiled
3. owner

4. confusion
5. story
6. clear

Part 3: Multiple Meaning Words

A.
1. b
2. b
3. b
4. a

5. b
6. a
7. a
8. b

Unit 6, Lesson 3

Part 1: Idioms

A.
1. H
2. G
3. J
4. L
5. K
6. C

7. B
8. I
9. D
10. E
11. F
12. A

Part 2: Synonyms

Across
2. expression
5. jabbering
6. snarled
9. preference
11. distinct
12. proprietor

Down
1. whirled
3. narrative
4. personal
7. distract
8. pampered
10. chaos

Part 3: Multiple Meaning Words

A.
1. box
2. marble
3. watered
4. touched
5. check

Unit 6, Unit Test

Part A: Idioms

1. E
2. J
3. D
4. O
5. F
6. N
7. C
8. L
9. M
10. B
11. I
12. K
13. G
14. A
15. H

Part B: Synonyms

1. private
2. spoiled
3. story
4. liking
5. clear
6. look
7. owner
8. tangled
9. disturb
10. confusion

Part C: Multiple Meaning Words

1. mine
2. ight
3. face
4. touched
5. land

Unit 7, Lesson 1

Part 1: Idioms

A. 1. G
   2. B
   3. C
   4. D
   5. I

   6. G
   7. E
   8. F
   9. H
   10. A

Part 2: Specialized Vocabulary

A. 1. a competition among swimmers
   2. rows for each swimmer to swim in
   3. early races to establish who will compete in later races
   4. the later races in which the best swimmer are determined
   5. a swimmer who jumps into the water before the signal
   6. a race in which four swimmers make up a team and switch with each other during the race
   7. one who is trained to save lives in the water

Part 3: Context Clues

A. 1. shocked and confused
   2. too self-confident and bragging
   3. the body's ability to react quickly without thinking
   4. race tracks
   5. bold and always trying to get what one wants
   6. ad
   7. a legal agreement with someone else

Unit 7, Lesson 2

Part 1: Idioms

A. 1. D
   2. G
   3. A
   4. H
   5. B

   6. C
   7. F
   8. E
   9. G
   10. I

Part 2: Specialized Vocabulary

A. 1. roadway closed off for the purpose of racing
   2. a track shaped like an egg
   3. the mechanics who keep a car running
   4. when a driver pulls off the track to get the car fixed or refueled
   5. a large business or corporation that pays for something
   6. abels to advertise something
   7. seats around a track

Part 3: Context Clues

A. 1. a period of time
   2. set on fire
   3. to speak
   4. lose one's memory
   5. what is inside something
   6. way of joining metal together
   7. free time

Unit 7, Lesson 3

Part 1: Idioms

A. 1. J
   2. G
   3. H
   4. C
   5. I
   6. E

   7. L
   8. K
   9. B
   10. F
   11. A
   12. D

Part 2: Specialized Vocabulary

A. 1. grand stands
   2. logo
   3. sponsor
   4. time trials
   5. oval track
   6. pit stop
   7. crew

B. 1. swim meet
   2. life guard
   3. goggles
   4. heats
   5. finals
   6. relay
   7. false start

Part 3: Context Clues

A. 1. ignited
   2. pushy
   3. welded
   4. tracks
   5. leisure
   6. awkward
   7. contents
   8. interval

   9. reflexes
   10. amnesia
   11. depressed
   12. lack
   13. dazed
   14. contract
   15. cocky

Unit 7, Unit Test

Part A: Idioms

1. G
2. J
3. O
4. K
5. I
6. E
7. M
8. L
9. A
10. D
11. N
12. C
13. F
14. B
15. H

Part B Specialized Vocabulary

Across
2. logos
6. lanes
7. finals
9. sponsor
12. heat
13. crew

Down
1. relay
3. goggles
4. stands
5. pit stop
8. track
10. oval
11. meet

Part C: Context Clues

1. cocky
2. reflexes
3. oral
4. interval
5. depressed
6. contract
7. dazed
8. amnesia

Unit 8, Lesson 1

Part 1: Multiple-Meaning Words

A. 1. a   4. a
     2. b   5. b
     3. b   6. c

Part 2: Context Clues

A. 1. take secretly   4. interested
     2. hide   5. hurt
     3. careful   6. funny

Part 3: Compound Words

A. 1. bedroom
     2. sunlight
     3. coveralls
     4. fireplace
     5. floorboards

B. 1. bedroom   courtyard
     2. fireplace   outdoors
     3. sunlight   raincoat
     4. floorboards   driftwood
     5. coveralls   birthday
     6. sunlight   wide-awake
     7. coveralls   short-tempered
     8. fireplace   campground
     9. floorboards   grandmother
     10. bedroom   windowpane

Unit 8, Lesson 2

Part 1: Multiple-Meaning Words

A. 1. b   4. b
     2. b   5. a
     3. a   6. c

Part 2: Context Clues

A. 1. too   4. food
     2. changed   5. respect
     3. customer   6. even so

Part 3: Compound Words

A. 1. well-heeled   4. double-cross
     2. evil-looking   5. stopwatch
     3. fingerprint

B. 1. seventh-grader   10. double-cross
     2. teammates   11. outside
     3. cornfield   12. timekeeper
     4. barnyard   13. stopwatch
     5. half-mile   14. halfway
     6. mailbox   15. self-resepect
     7. well-heeled   16. small-town
     8. gunshot   17. wildcat
     9. twenty-third

Unit 8, Lesson 3

Part 1: Multiple-Meaning Words

A. 1. spare
2. hide
3. wake
4. tag

Part 2: Context Clues

A. 1. food
2. interested
3. too
4. respect
5. careful
6. hide

Part 3: Compound Words

Across
5. fireplace
7. bedroom
8. fingerprint
9. outdoors

Down
1. stopwatch
2. barnyard
3. mailbox
4. teammates
5. floorboards
6. coveralls

Unit 8, Unit Test

Part A: Multiple-Meaning Words

1. crane
2. wake
3. spare
4. thick
5. spring

Part B: Context Clues

1. client
2. conceal
3. nourishment
4. modified
5. intrigued
6. comical
7. smuggle
8. thorough

Part C: Compound Words

1. I
2. A
3. H
4. N
5. F
6. J
7. O
8. M
9. D
10. E
11. C
12. L
13. B
14. G
15. K

Unit 9, Lesson 1

Part 1: Prefixes

A. 1. super/human – one with abilities beyond normal human abilities
2. con/form – to do what others are doing
3. trans/plant – to move from one place to another
4. ir/regular – not regular or normal
5. sub/marine – a vessel designed to move under water
6. col/lapse – to fall down
7. super/charge – to increase the power of something, such as an engine
8. com/mit – to agree to do something
9. ir/responsible – not responsible or reliable
10. trans/port – to carry something to a new destination
11. cor/respond – to write a letter
12. sub/way – a transportation system underneath a city

Part 2: Greek and Latin Roots

A. 1. E
2. H
3. G
4. B
5. A
6. K
7. F
8. J
9. D
10. C

Part 3: Shades of Meaning

A. 1. C
2. B
3. A
4. C

Unit 9, Lesson 2

Part 1: Suffixes

A. 1. confid/ence – the state of being confident; self-assured
2. same/ness – the state of being alike
3. rac/ism – a hatred of others because of their racial origin
4. brother/hood – a belief or feeling in caring for others
5. depend/ence – the state of needing or depending on another
6. real/ism – the representation of things as they naturally appear
7. defi/ance – the act of defying or revolting
8. stud/ent – one who studies
9. mother/hood – the state of being a mother, usually with children
10. obedi/ence – the act of obeying or doing as another says
11. abund/ance – the state of great wealth
12. resid/ence – a home

Part 2: Greek and Latin Roots

A. 1. K   6. J
2. C   7. D
3. A   8. F
4. H   9. B
5. G   10. E

Part 3: Shades of Meaning

A. 1. B   3. C
2. C   4. A

Unit 9, Lesson 3

Part 1: Prefixes

A. 1. I   7. E
2. L   8. B
3. G   9. K
4. A   10. F
5. J   11. D
6. C   12. H

Part 2: Greek and Latin Roots

A. 1. mech/anic   8. trans/form
2. in/spect   9. therm/al
3. tele/scope   10. re/cede
4. dis/rupt   11. therm/os
5. re/cess   12. tele/phoned
6. spect/acles   13. suc/ceed
7. tract/or

Part 3: Shades of Meaning

A. 1. C
2. A
3. C
4. D

Unit 9, Unit Test

Part A: Prefixes and Suffixes

1. b
2. i
3. o
4. r
5. a
6. i
7. l
8. p
9. e
10. g

Part B: Greek and Latin Roots

1. D
2. G
3. H
4. E
5. L
6. C
7. K
8. F
9. B
10. I
11. A
12. J

1. B
2. A
3. A
4. A
5. B
6. B
7. B
8. A

Part C: Shades of Meaning

1. C
2. C
3. D
4. A
5. B

Unit 10, Lesson 1

Part 1: Multiple-Meaning Words

A. 1. b
2. c
3. b
4. c
5. b
6. a

Part 2: Context Clues

A. 1. escaped
2. bravery
3. lies
4. firm
5. shortage of food
6. begged

Part 3: Using a Dictionary

A. 1. noun – an account of an event or series of events
2. noun – a long, slender rounded piece of wood or other material
3. noun – a thick growth of bushes and shrubs
4. verb – to seek safety or refuge
5. noun – the skin of an animal

Unit 10, Lesson 2

Part 1: Multiple-Meaning Words

A. 1. c
2. b
3. a
4. b
5. c
6. a

Part 2: Context Clues

A. 1. small
2. brace
3. wild
4. planned
5. food
6. machine that kills germs

Part 3: Using a Dictionary

A. 1. verb – to deal or cope with
2. noun – a small, pointed device used for sewing or surgery
3. adjective – having a sharp rise or incline
4. noun – a piece of cloth, usually canvas, spread across a wooden frame for the sick or wounded
5. verb – to tease or provoke

Unit 10, Lesson 3

Part 1: Multiple-Meaning Words

A. 1. c
2. b
3. c
4. b
5. b

Part 2: Context Clues

A. 1. small
2. planned
3. brace
4. firm
5. shortage of food
6. begged

Part 3: Using a Dictionary

A. 1. noun – a part that is designed to be held
2. noun – account of an event
3. noun – the set of rooms on the same level of a building
4. verb – to soak in liquid in order to clean
5. verb – to put or keep out of sight

Unit 10, Unit Test

Part A: Multiple-Meaning Words

1. skirt
2. check
3. deed
4. watch
5. arms

Part B: Context Clues

1 runaway
2. courage
3. intended
4. falsehood
5. raging
6. determined
7. steep
8. implored

Part C: Using a Dictionary

1. verb – to touch, lift, or hold with the hands
2. noun – the skin of an animal
3. verb – to clean, polish, or scrub with a brush
4. adjective – having a sharp rise or incline
5. noun – a piece of cloth, usually canvas, spread across a wooden frame for the sick or wounded
6. noun – an account of an event or series of events

Unit 11, Lesson 1

Part 1: Homophones

A.
1. for
2. wear
3. band
4. reins
5. four
6. gait
7. roll
8. waist
9. to
10. When

Part 2: Greek and Latin Roots

A.
1. G
2. J
3. D
4. E
5. I
6. A
7. B
8. H
9. F
10. C

Part 3: Syllabication

A.
1. win + ner   3
2. light + weight   1
3. cheer + ing   2
4. de + cide   5
5. pub + lic   4
6. loud + ly   2
7. cab + in   6

Unit 11, Lesson 2

Part 1: Homophones

A.
1. born
2. past
3. site
4. mourn
5. bawl
6. wring
7. foul
8. Through
9. cheap
10. owe

Part 2: Greek and Latin Roots

A.
1. E
2. D
3. I
4. B
5. C
6. A
7. F
8. J
9. G
10. H

Part 3: Syllabication

A.
1. him + self   1
2. mil + lion   3
3. al + most   4
4. writ + er   5
5. grave + yard   1
6. out + doors   1
7. sev + en   6
8. sad + dest   3
9. de + fend   5
10. bod + ies   6
11. slow + ly   2
12. prov + ince   6

Unit 11, Lesson 3

Part 1: Homophones

A.
1. fowl
2. sight
3. gate
4. rains
5. roll
6. waist
7. band
8. morn

B. Fluency
1. Win – When
2. threw – through
3. fowl – foul
4. Wear – Where
5. ring – wring
6. past – passed
7. site – sight
8. waist – waste
9. gate – gait
10. two – to
11. cheep – cheap
12. band – banned
13. for – four
14. Owe – Oh

Part 2: Greek and Latin Roots

A.
1. B
2. A
3. D
4. F
5. E
6. C

B.
1. junction
2. audiotape
3. gracious
4. gratify
5. fragment
6. cardiac
7. optical
8. defect
9. factory

Part 3: Syllabication

A.
1. mil + lion   3
2. light + weight   1
3. slow + ly   2
4. de + cide   5
5. pub + lic   4
6. mag + ic   6
7. cab + in   6
8. al + most   4

Unit 11, Unit Test

Part A: Homophones

1. c
2. g
3. m
4. t
5. b
6. h
7. n
8. r
9. d
10. g

Part B: Greek and Latin Roots

1. L
2. C
3. B
4. J
5. A
6. K
7. E
8. D
9. I
10. F
11. G
12. H

1. A
2. A
3. B
4. A
5. B
6. B
7. B
8. B

Part C: Syllabication

1. out + doors
2. slow + ly
3. frag + ment
4. de + cide
5. mil + lion
6. op + ti + cal
7. light + weight
8. cab + in
9. writ + er
10. loud + ly
11. fac + to + ry
12. sev + en
13. sad + dest
14. base + ball
15. bod + ies
16. al + most
17. grat + i + fy
18. him + self
19. prov + ince
20. pub + lic

Unit 12, Lesson 1

Part 1: Idioms

A.
1. F
2. C
3. B
4. G
5. J
6. H
7. E
8. D
9. I
10. A

Part 2: Context Clues

A.
1. to become violent and very angry
2. disgust
3. to yell loudly like a wild animal
4. a large house surrounded by a lot of land
5. someone from another country
6. a secret plan
7. to trick someone
8. to behave

Part 3: Structural Analysis

A.
1. quickly
2. toward
3. daily
4. secretly
5. globally
6. lengthwise
7. automatically
8. sleepily
9. crazily
10. typically
11. frantically
12. seaward

Unit 12, Lesson 2

Part 1: Idioms

A.
1. H
2. G
3. A
4. D
5. B
6. C
7. E
8. G
9. F
10. I

Part 2: Context Clues

A.
1. a small, hard object
2. stray hair
3. a small insect that flies
4. as a result
5. a small piece of hair
6. announcement
7. a course in science of how things work
8. something said

Part 3: Structural Analysis

A.
1. player
2. machinist
3. occupant
4. engineer
5. beautician
6. inspector
7. racist
8. builder
9. auctioneer
10. conductor
11. mathematician
12. geologist

Unit 12, Lesson 3

Part 1: Idioms

A. 1. F
    2. A
    3. D
    4. E
    5. C
    6. B
    7. H
    8. G

B. 1. a bad apple
    2. going bananas
    3. pay him any mind
    4. take it easy
    5. in the dog house
    6. have their eyes on him
    7. in the long run

Part 2: Context Clues

A. 1. announcement
    2. grand home with a lot of land
    3. something said
    4. tricks
    5. someone from another country
    6. angry reaction

Part 3: Structural Analysis

A. 1. F
    2. G
    3. C
    4. I
    5. A
    6. J
    7. E
    8. B
    9. H
    10. D

Unit 12, Test

Part A: Idioms

1. B
2. A
3. J
4. F
5. L
6. N
7. O
8. G
9. M
10. K
11. H
12. E
13. D
14. C
15. I

Part B: Context Clues

1. foreigner
2. utterances
3. tantrum
4. double-crossed
5. bulletin
6. estate
7. horror
8. plot

Part C: Structural Anlaysis

Across
2. dietician
4. counselor
5. mountaineer
6. seaward
8. frantically
9. engineer
10. auctioneer

Down
1. machinist
3. occupant
4. commandant
7. globally
8. foreigner

Greek and Latin Roots
Used In PowerWords

aero means "air"
anthrop means "human"
aud means "hear"
auto means "self, alone"
bibl and *biblio* mean "books"
bio means "life"
capt and *cept* mean "take, have"
cardi means "heart"
cede, ceed, and *cess* mean "go, yield, give away"
chron means "time"
cycl means "circle, ring"
dem means "people"
dic or *dict* mean "speak, say, tell"
div means "separate"
doc means "teach"
duc and *duct* mean "lead"
equi means "equal"
fact and *fect* mean "do, make"
flect or *flex* mean "bend"
fer means "carry, bear"
form means "form or shape"
fract and *frag* mean "break"
funct means "perform"
gen means "birth, race, kind"
geo means "earth"
grad means "step, stage"
graph and *gram* mean "write, draw, describe"
grat and *grac* mean "pleasing"
hydr means "water"
ject means "throw, hurl"
jud means "judge"
junct means "join"
liber means "free"
loc and *locat* mean "place"
log means "word, reason, study"
mech means "machine"
mem and *ment* mean "mind"
meter and *metr* mean "measure"
miss and *mit* mean "send"
mob, mot, and *mov* mean "move"
mort means "death"

Greek and Latin Roots
Used In PowerWords continued

neo means "new"

nom and *nym* mean "name, word, law"

not means "note, mark"

opt means "visible"

ortho means "straight, correct"

para means "get ready"

pel and *puls* mean "drive, thrust, urge, throb"

phil means "love"

phob means "fear"

phon means "sound"

photo means "light"

phys means "nature"

poli means "city"

pon, pos, and *posit* mean "place, put"

port means "carry"

psych means "mind, soul, spirit"

ques means "ask, seek"

rupt means "break"

schola means "school"

scop and *skept* mean "look at, examine"

scope means "see"

scrib or *script* mean "write"

sens or *sent* mean "feel"

soph means "wise"

spec, spect, and *spic* mean "look, see"

tain, ten, and *tent* mean "hold"

techn means "art, skill"

tele means "far, distant"

theo means "god"

therm means "heat"

trac and *tract* mean "pull, move"

turb means "confusion"

var means "different"

ven and *vent* mean "come"

vert or *ver* mean "turn"

voc means "voice, call"

volv means "roll"

vid or *vis* mean "see"

Appendix B

Homophones Used In PowerWords

<table>
<tr><td>be/bee</td><td>blue/blew</td><td>no/know</td></tr>
<tr><td>here/hear</td><td>to/too/two</td><td>hi/high</td></tr>
<tr><td>new/knew</td><td>see/sea</td><td>there/they're/their</td></tr>
<tr><td>bear/bare</td><td>by/buy/bye</td><td>deer/dear</td></tr>
<tr><td>ate/eight</td><td>for/four/fore</td><td>our/hour</td></tr>
<tr><td>red/read</td><td>lead/led</td><td>meat/meet</td></tr>
<tr><td>plane/plain</td><td>rode/road/rowed</td><td>sail/sale</td></tr>
<tr><td>stare/stair</td><td>we'll/wheel</td><td>hole/whole</td></tr>
<tr><td>wear/ware/where</td><td>one/won</td><td>flower/flour</td></tr>
<tr><td>right/write</td><td>your/you're</td><td>its/it's</td></tr>
<tr><td>not/knot</td><td>gate/gait</td><td>time/thyme</td></tr>
<tr><td>son/sun</td><td>hey/hay</td><td>made/maid</td></tr>
<tr><td>male/mail</td><td>nay/neigh</td><td>oh/owe</td></tr>
<tr><td>pail/pale</td><td>peek/peak</td><td>reed/read</td></tr>
<tr><td>so/sew/sow</td><td>root/route</td><td>shone/shown</td></tr>
<tr><td>break/brake</td><td>cent/sent/scent</td><td>flee/flea</td></tr>
<tr><td>creak/creek</td><td>die/dye</td><td>fair/fare</td></tr>
<tr><td>hair/hare</td><td>heard/herd</td><td>night/knight</td></tr>
<tr><td>steel/steal</td><td>tail/tale</td><td>thrown/throne</td></tr>
<tr><td>fir/fur</td><td>waist/waste</td><td>week/weak</td></tr>
<tr><td>we've/weave</td><td>way/weigh</td><td>wait/weight</td></tr>
<tr><td>threw/through</td><td>aisle/I'll</td><td>ball/bawl</td></tr>
<tr><td>beat/beet</td><td>course/coarse</td><td>cheap/cheep</td></tr>
<tr><td>days/daze</td><td>doe/dough</td><td>heel/heal</td></tr>
<tr><td>do/dew/due</td><td>in/inn</td><td>need/knead</td></tr>
<tr><td>lone/loan</td><td>ring/wring</td><td>pole/poll</td></tr>
<tr><td>earn/urn</td><td>past/passed</td><td>sweet/suite</td></tr>
<tr><td>ore/or</td><td>rain/reign/rein</td><td>role/roll</td></tr>
<tr><td>sole/soul</td><td>seller/cellar</td><td>soar/sore</td></tr>
<tr><td>steak/stake</td><td>some/sum</td><td>tow/toe</td></tr>
<tr><td>vein/vane/vain</td><td>medal/metal</td><td>tea/tee</td></tr>
<tr><td>great/grate</td><td>poor/pour</td><td>haul/hall</td></tr>
<tr><td>piece/peace</td><td>flair/flare</td><td>mist/missed</td></tr>
<tr><td>mane/main</td><td>wail/whale</td><td>died/dyed</td></tr>
<tr><td>manor/manner</td><td>pier/peer</td><td>rap/wrap</td></tr>
<tr><td>maze/maize</td><td>air/heir</td><td>prays/praise</td></tr>
<tr><td>base/bass</td><td>wade/weighed</td><td>knave/nave</td></tr>
<tr><td>bread/bred</td><td>guessed/guest</td><td>real/reel</td></tr>
<tr><td>sees/seas</td><td>feet/feat</td><td>humn/him</td></tr>
<tr><td>scents/sense/cents</td><td>tents/tense</td><td>sight/site</td></tr>
<tr><td>fined/find</td><td>side/sighed</td><td>tide/tied</td></tr>
<tr><td>paws/pause</td><td>born/borne</td><td>chord/cord</td></tr>
<tr><td>foul/fowl</td><td>mourn/morn</td><td></td></tr>
</table>

Prefixes Used in PowerWords

a- and *ab-* mean "up," "out," "away," or "not"
anti- means "against"
be- means "cause to become" or "about"
bene- means "good"
bi- means "two"
circum- means "around"
co- means "together, equally, jointly"
col-, com-, con-, and *cor-* mean "with" or "together"
contra- means "opposed" or "against"
counter- means "opposite" or "contrary"
de- means "make the opposite of"
dis- means "not" or "lack of"
em- and *en-* mean "in," "into," or "to make or cause"
ex- means "out" or "former"
extra- means "outside"
fore- means "before" or "earlier"
hyper- means "more than normal"
im-, il-, and *in-* mean "not"
inter- means "among" or "between"
intra- means "within"
ir- means "not"
mal- means "bad"
mid- means "halfway"
mis- means "wrong" or "wrongly"
mono- means "one"
multi- means "many"
non- means "not"
omni- means "all"
over- means "above" or "superior"
post- means "after" or "later"
pre- means "before"
pro- means "forward"
re- means "again" or "back"
self- means "oneself" or "automatic"
semi- means "half"
sub- means "below"
super- means "above" or "beyond"
trans- means "across"
tri- means "three"
un- means "not" or "the opposite of"
uni- means "one"

Suffixes Used in Power Words

-*able/-ible* means "wanting to" or "able to be"

-*al* means "relating to"

-*ance* turns a word or word part into a noun

-*ant* and -*ist* mean "one who does something"

-*ate* means "having" or "full of"

-*ation, -ion, -sion,* and -*ment* mean "a state or quality of"

-*ence* turns a word or word part into a noun

-*er* means "more" or "more than" (comparative)

-*est* means "the most" (superlative)

-*fy* or -*ify* means "to make"

-*ful* means "full of" or "having"

-*hood* turns a word or word part into a noun

-*ise* or -*ize* means "to become"

-*ious/-ous* means "possessing" or "full of"

-*ism* turns a word or word part into a noun

-*less* means "without" or "lacking"

-*ness* turns a word or word part into a noun

-*some* means "likely to"

-*ways* means "in what manner"

Rules for Syllabication

When a word is composed of two complete words (a compound word), divide between the two words.

      cork • screw   fire • place   war • plane
      fence • post   girl • friend   light • weight

When there are identical consonants between vowels, the word is divided between consonants.

      big • ger   cor • rect   rab • bit
      suf • fer   sum • mer   win • ner

Prefixes and suffixes generally form separate syllables.

      dis • arm   mis • read   quick • ly
      try • ing   un • do   un • friend • ly

When there is one consonant between two vowel sounds, the consonant usually goes with the second syllable, if the preceding vowel is long.

      be • hind   be • lieve   de • cide
      pho • to   pi • lot   si • lence

When there is one consonant between two vowel sounds, the consonant usually goes with the first syllable, if the vowel is short.

      nev • er   pet • al   prof • it
      mod • el   cab • in   fin • ish

Accent Generalizations

The accent usually falls on or within the root word of a word containing a prefix and/or a suffix.

   re play'   truth' ful   dis able'   cool' est

In a compound word, the primary accent usually falls on, or within, the first word.

   air' plane   fire' place   wheel' chair   up' stairs

In a two-syllable word that functions as either a noun or verb, the accent is usually on the first syllable when the word is used as a noun, and the second syllable when the word functions as a verb.

   pre' sent   pre sent'   con' tract   con tract'

When there is a double consonant within a word, the accent usually falls on the syllable which ends with the first letter of the double consonant.

   snug' gle   din' ner   mat' ter   rab' bit

In a multi-syllabic word ending in "ion" the primary accent falls on the syllable preceding the "ion" ending.

   re la' tion   ed u ca' tion

When the last syllable of a word is composed of two vowel letters, that syllable is usually accented.

   com pose'   con tain'

When there is no other clue in a two-syllable word, the accent most often falls on the first syllable.

Dolch List of Sight Words

a
about
after
again
all
am
an
and
any
are
around
as
ask
at
ate
away
be
because
been
before
best
better
big
black
blue
both
bring
brown
but
buy
by
call
came
can
carry
clean
cold
come
could
cut

did
does
done
don't
down
draw
drink
eat
eight
every
fall
far
fast
find
first
five
fly
for
found
four
from
full
funny
gave
get
give
go
goes
going
good
got
green
grow
had
has
have
he
help
here
him

his
hold
hot
how
hurt
I
if
in
into
is
it
its
jump
just
keep
kind
know
laugh
let
light
like
little
live
long
look
made
make
many
may
me
much
must
myself
never
new
no
not
now
of

old
on
once
one
only
open
or
our
out
over
own
pick
play
please
pretty
pull
put
ran
read
red
ride
right
round
run
said
saw
see
seven
she
show
sing
sit

six
sleep
small
so
some
soon
start
stop
take
tell
ten
thank
that
the
their
them
then
there
these
they
think
this
those
three
to
today
together
too
try
two
up
upon

us
use

very
walk
want
warm
was
wash
we
well
went
were
what
when
where
which
white
who
why
will
wish
with
work
would
write
yellow
yes
you
your